SNUFF BOXES

SNUFF BOXES

KENNETH BLAKEMORE

FREDERICK MULLER LIMITED
LONDON

First published in Great Britain 1976
by Frederick Muller Limited, London NW2 6LE

ISBN 0 584 10269 0

Printed in Great Britain by The Anchor Press Ltd
and bound by Wm Brendon & Son Ltd
both of Tiptree, Essex

CONTENTS

CONTENTS

COLOUR ILLUSTRATIONS

BLACK AND WHITE ILLUSTRATIONS

To Gerald Sanders
for his unfailing helpfulness.

PREFACE

Perhaps one of the reasons that people find snuff boxes so fascinating is just because they are small boxes, for we are always
intrigued by the miniature, impressed by the craftsmanship
implicit in a *tour de force* on a small scale. But there is another
explanation of the obvious attraction these boxes have for the
casual visitor to museums and to the dedicated collector alike.
Many people sense the associations of these boxes, even if they are
not fully aware of them. They have an ability to evoke, particularly those exquisite confections wrought from gold now housed
in the famous collections, a mode of life remote from ours, a period
that seems in retrospect more romantic and more leisured than
the mundane present in which we are condemned to live. These
boxes belong to a period that seems strangely mannered to us,
when etiquette was no mere formality but a way of life. They
recall the Versailles of Louis XV. They call to mind Strawberry
Hill where Horace Walpole built his rococo grotto and wrote
letters interminably. They conjure up that strange court of the
schizophrenic Frederick the Great, the St Petersburg of those
amorous Empresses of Russia, and Bath under the spell of Beau
Nash. Sacheverell Sitwell wrote that "we have the memory of
those who handled them so that they become little personal
things of ghostly evocation".[1]

If these boxes impress those who study them today because they
were once the treasured possessions or the considered gifts of
kings, the baubles of famous courtesans and the perquisites of
courtiers, they cannot fail to impress us also with the virtuosity of
those who fashioned them. They are, to quote Sacheverell Sitwell
again: "the result of a series of technical processes any one of
which would form a skilled profession in itself." At their finest
they are "among the most lovely and entrancing objects made by
human hands." And even when they are not fashioned from gold
and decked out with enamels and gems, or formed from tortoise-

[1] Sitwell, Sacheverell, Preface to *Eighteenth-Century Gold Boxes of Europe*, Kenneth
Snowman, Faber and Faber, 1966.

shell scattered with bright points of piqué, but made from humbler substances such as bone or wood or pinchbeck or Sheffield plate, they are nonetheless the result of much hard-won skill and many tedious hours of application. And when one thinks about it, how incredible it was that so many men spent whole lifetimes bent over their benches, catering to perhaps the strangest of all strange human foibles, the sniffing of a few grains of tobacco from a box.

There is no question that, at the height of this curious fashion, the container for the snuff was as important as the *de rigueur* habit of snuffing itself. The box had an essential part to play in that little formal ballet of hands and fingers which the accomplished snuffer managed so expertly. The box told the onlooker as much about the man as did his skill in carrying the snuff to his nose. It revealed his position, his wealth and his taste. These boxes were above all else status symbols and kings and queens, mistresses and ambassadors sometimes acquired as many snuff boxes as there were days in a year, and some, like Frederick the Great and Count Heinrich von Brühl, died owning many times that number. Nor were men and women of lesser means content with a single box.

Nowadays when relatively few people take snuff, there are still those who collect boxes as avidly as Madame de Pompadour and Catherine the Great collected them. It can be an expensive hobby. A single fine enamelled box by a Paris maker like Jean George or Jean Ducrollay could cost a collector £40,000 or more. But one of the attractions of snuff box collecting is that it can be indulged in at any level. While no antiques are cheap these days, a man of modest means can acquire an interesting collection of snuff boxes if he is prepared to seek for beautiful or interesting examples in less rarefied areas. One can buy very attractive nineteenth-century silver boxes for between £50 and £200, and eighteenth-century silver-mounted boxes for even less. Then there are the painted enamel boxes, papier-mâché boxes, boxes of pressed horn and boxes fashioned from a variety of woods. The choice is infinite. Even when one has looked at thousands of snuff boxes there are still surprises in store, new discoveries to be made, new enigmas to be pondered, new additions to be made to one's collection.

But, of course, one does not have to collect snuff boxes to enjoy them. One can study them as part of our heritage, as intriguing fragments of our past, in the great museums and in private collections. Even the small museums sometimes have fascinating examples of the art of the smallworkers of the past to show the visitors with a few minutes to spare. Thus snuff box hunting can easily become, as it has for me, such an absorbing hobby that one never passes even the grubbiest of antique shops without peering hopefully into the windows.

In writing a book as wide ranging as this, one inevitably draws upon those who have in the past explored various aspects of the subject, some of whom have spent many years researching just one facet of it. I should like therefore to acknowledge my indebtedness to all those who have written about snuff boxes, and in particular those authors whose works are listed in the short bibliography at the back of this book. When I set out to write this book, however, I decided that wherever possible I would go back to source. I came to this decision for two reasons. For one thing the literature on snuff boxes is still far from comprehensive. Secondly, as a onetime student of F. R. Leavis, I had it drummed into me that one should always go to the text and form one's own opinions. In this instance the texts are the snuff boxes themselves, and I have made a point of looking at thousands of snuff boxes in museums and private collections, and where the actual boxes were not available I have studied photographs of them. This research has served sometimes only to confirm accepted opinions, but in other instances it has led me to question the theories that others have advanced, and I think I have made one or two "discoveries" that seem to have been overlooked by my predecessors in the field.

What I have found particularly fascinating in researching this book has been to discover that there is still so much that is unexplained. Because of the absence of marks on most boxes, or of any other external evidence, the dating and the attribution of many boxes are sometimes difficult, often impossible. All one has are the shape and decoration of the box, the type of hinge and thumbpiece to guide one. And there are many traps for the unwary in dating on the basis of appearance alone. For instance, at certain periods souvenir boxes were popular, adorned with portraits of monarchs who had been long dead. There is, for example, a large English oval tortoise-shell box made either for smoking tobacco or for snuff, with ring piqué arranged in little triangles round the rim of the fluted lid, and with a pierced silver plaque in the centre depicting Charles II. Ring piqué in this form may well have been used to decorate tortoise-shell in the Charles II period, but this box is so like the pressed horn boxes of Obrisset that one feels certain that it could not have been made before the first decade of the eighteenth century.

In describing this box it will have been noted that I hesitated to describe it as definitely a snuff box. One does not know for certain, in many instances, for what particular purpose boxes were designed. Little boxes were made to contain many things in the past—patches, sweetmeats, spices, toothpicks, surgical instruments and gambling counters among other things. Often the intended use is obvious, yet often it is not. For instance, those little oval boxes from the Charles II period, usually with amatory designs and inscriptions engraved on them, have been described as spice boxes. Perhaps they were intended for spice, but no one has advanced any conclusive evidence of the fact. They would have been very suitable for snuff-taking, being easy to hold, thumb and finger pressed on the silver discs soldered on either end of them. It has been suggested that these little boxes were too small for snuff boxes, but the reason why many boxes from this period are thought to have been tobacco boxes is because they are considered to be too big for snuff. In fact well documented snuff boxes have, over the centuries, been made in all sizes as well as in all shapes, from the unbelievably big to the incredibly small.

Another fascinating area, where doubts will probably never be resolved and opinions never confirmed by documentation, is the source of decoration. There was much more communication between countries in the seventeenth and eighteenth centuries than we often imagine. Those who designed boxes in one country were far from working in isolation. Artists uprooted by religious intolerance or merely seeking to make their fortune in another country, settled in London or in Amsterdam or in Stockholm. These expatriate craftsmen not only produced boxes in the manner in which they had been taught by their master in their native country, but meeting with some commercial success they influenced the craftsmen of their adoptive country to copy their work. Also there were designs and pattern books that could be bought, and as we know from studying Scandinavian rococo boxes, actual castings that could be bought in from abroad, incorporated in a box lid and chased up. Some subjects were universally popular throughout Europe: the *fêtes champêtres* of Watteau and Lancret were as popular in England and Germany as they were in France, and engravings "after Watteau" provided motifs that were copied on the Hausmalerei and were painted in enamel on copper in Birmingham, Bilston and Wednesbury.

During the period between the middle of the seventeenth century and the middle of the nineteenth century, snuff boxes were produced all over Europe. France, Germany and England were by far the most important producer nations, with the Scandinavian countries, Russia and Switzerland also supporting considerable box-making industries. Some fine boxes were produced in Austria and Holland, too. Surprisingly, we have almost no boxes from Spain, the cradle of the courtly habit of snuffing. In the words of Clare le Corbeiller, "Despite the pre-eminence of Spain in the consumption and manufacture of snuff, the production of boxes in any material appears to have been wholly insignificant."[1] My own researches and enquiries have only served to confirm Miss Corbeiller's statement. And what is true of Spain is also, equally surprisingly, true of Italy where snuffing was fashionable at an early date. The few boxes of Italian provenance that do exist are so varied that no worthwhile conclusions can be drawn from them about Italian styles or Italian makers.

Outside Europe there was a small production in America, though in the eighteenth century many of the American snuffers imported European boxes. Then from the seventeenth century to the present day there has been a thriving industry in China, producing those little snuff bottles from natural materials and man-made ones.

It can be seen that very often in writing about snuff boxes one is expressing opinions rather than stating facts. The question of beauty too is very much a matter of opinion. I have always

[1] le Corbeiller, Clare, *European and American Snuff Boxes*, London, 1966.

believed, however, that "old" and "beautiful" are not, as some people obviously feel they are, synonymous terms. Antiques are not always beautiful. Sometimes they are downright ugly and often in rather doubtful taste, even allowing for the fact that the atrocities of one age can be the sublimities of another. One has to accept, I think, that some very bad snuff boxes were made in the past, boxes of poor workmanship and weak design. Many of the japanned iron boxes have, I feel, little to recommend them. Most of the brass boxes I have seen leave me unimpressed, and the few surviving pewter boxes are without exception horrible. Nor can I generate much enthusiasm for many of the painted and printed enamel boxes made in England, Germany and Scandinavia. Too often they betray the fact that they were painted by men of little talent working at sweat-shop rates in the stygian gloom of miserable workshops.

On the other hand some of the snuff boxes of the past are unbelievably beautiful. They transcend craftsmen and must, I believe, be considered as works of art. I am thinking for instance of the chased gold boxes of Gouers, Moser and Bergs, and the enamelled boxes of George, Ducrollay and Hardivilliers. And certainly one must include in this category the best of the Chinese snuff bottles and the finest of the piqué-decorated tortoise-shell boxes.

Between the two extremes of the golden arts at their finest and the ugly and the ill-made, there are the thousands of boxes which have beauty, charm, or some feature of unusual interest to recommend them to the collector and the connoisseur.

In treating so large and varied a subject in a single book, I found myself in the situation of having to select for illustration and discussion only those snuff containers which I thought best represented the various periods and the various techniques of manufacture. Like any compiler of an anthology, I have had to miss out some of my favourite pieces and no doubt other people's favourites too. For every box that I have illustrated here or have mentioned there are hundreds that might have taken their place, and it would be possible to expand every section of this book into a volume in its own right. The world of the snuff box is a vast one. When I told a friend of mine that I was doing a book on this subject, he asked me whether I thought I would find enough to write about. The problem has been, in fact, to select from the mass of material available and reduce the subject to readable proportions.

KENNETH BLAKEMORE

PART ONE

CHAPTER ONE

TOBACCO COMES TO EUROPE

In the year 1492 somewhere in the West Indies, two of the sailors from Columbus's tiny flotilla watched a party of Indians puffing away at rolled-up bundles of leaves. When in the following year one of these sailors, Rodrigo de Jerez, had landed safely back in Spain, he recounted this odd incident from an eventful voyage to the townspeople of Ayamonte. The Inquisition promptly threw him into jail for "consorting with the devil". The inquisitors had instinctively recognised a new sin with which they must wrestle.

As more and more Europeans beat their tiny ships across the stormy Atlantic to the New World in search of gold, they discovered that all over Central and Southern America the Indians gathered the big veiny leaves of the indigenous tobacco plant. Having cured these in the sun the Indians employed them in religious rituals, or used them to cure the sick, or set fire to them and inhaled the smoke just for the feeling of well-being this produced.

Bernal Díaz was one of that little band of conquistadors who was with Cortez when he miraculously overthrew the vast Aztec Empire. Díaz described how the Aztec king, Montezuma, after he had eaten would have placed before him "three tubes much painted and gilded, in which they put liquid amber mixed with some herbs which are called tobacco". This practice of smoking tobacco was no new Aztec fad. As later explorers were to discover, it had been practised perhaps a thousand years earlier by the predecessors of the Aztecs, the Maya. Mayan sculptors carved on the walls of their temples reliefs showing priests smoking pipes. A well preserved one can be seen at Palenque, depicting a priest wearing the skin of a jaguar and puffing contentedly on a pipe, probably as part of some religious ceremony.

When in 1532 Francisco Pizarro, with another small band of conquistadors, overthrew that other mighty civilisation of the

Americas, the Incas, it was discovered that they too used tobacco. But the Incas did not set fire to the dried leaves and inhale the fragrant smoke as the Aztecs did; they powdered the tobacco and sniffed this powder up their nostrils. They did this, it is recounted, both for the pleasure of it and because they found it relieved the catarrh which was prevalent among these people of the Altiplano. Tobacco was sufficiently important to these Peruvian people for the puppet-king Manco to give his son and heir the name Sagre-Tapac, meaning royal tobacco. The Incas probably did not invent the habit, later to become known as sniffing or snuffing, any more than the Aztecs invented smoking. They probably inherited it from those earlier Peruvian civilisations, the Chavin or the Chimu, from whom most of their culture derived.

Just how long it was after its discovery among the Indians, before their European conquerors adopted the strange habits of smoking and snuffing tobacco, is not known with any certainty. Certainly the habits were finding a foothold in Europe by the middle of the sixteenth century. Ramon Pane, a monk who accompanied Columbus's second expedition in 1493, is supposed to have brought seeds of the tobacco plant back to Spain, where the plant was later established. It seems that Pane had seen Indians snuffing tobacco in yet another area of the American continent, in Haiti. Pietro Martine d'Anghieri in his *De Orbe Novo Decades*, translated into English by Richard Eden in 1555, based his account of the Taino Indians snuffing tobacco on Pane's experience. The kings of these people were observed "snuffinge up into theyr nose-thryls the powder of the herbe called Corobba".

In 1559 the French Ambassador to the Court of Portugal, Jean Nicot, sent a gift of tobacco leaves and seeds to Catherine de Medici with instructions for their culture and use, and explained the plant's efficacy as a medicament. It is thought he may have obtained these from the botanist Damiao de Goes, who grew the plant in his garden in Lisbon. Whatever the source of his supply, Nicot was certainly responsible for making Catherine de Medici Europe's first royal snuff-taker, and his name has been associated with tobacco ever since.

In England, to begin with, tobacco was a sailor's vice. In 1556 a Bristol seaman had created some consternation when he had walked through the streets of the city "emitting smoke from his nostrils". He may not have been the first man in England to smoke, but the sight of him doing so was at this time unusual enough to attract comment. By 1570 Matthias de l'Obel and Petrus Pena could record the tact that tobacco was already being grown in England. And by this date too, Hawkins had already introduced the habit at court. As for Sir Walter Raleigh, at one time credited in the school books with introducing tobacco into England, he may well have had something to do with its general acceptance in court circles, but it was known in England long before his voyages to the Americas.

The earliest reference to snuffing in England is probably that in Harrison's *Chronicle* to "the taking-in of the finely pulverised Indian herb called tabaco by an instrument formed like a little ladel", and the fact that such a ladle was being specially produced at this time, 1580, suggests that the habit of snuff-taking was already an established one. By 1584 Queen Elizabeth thought this new vice of taking tobacco in one form or another was getting out of hand, and she issued a decree condemning its use. This was to be the first of many regal condemnations. It seems too, that at some time in Elizabeth's reign a duty of twopence a pound was levied on tobacco.

Tobacco already had its critics among the writers of the time. Henry Buttes averred that tobacco "mortifieth and benummeth: Causeth drownsinesse; troubleth and dulleth the sences". After Elizabeth's decree and duty came the censorious counterblast of James I against "this filthie noveltie, a great vanitie and un-cleanliness, a sinful and shameful lust . . ." Appreciating perhaps that the English were not greatly influenced by rhetoric, he increased the tax to six shillings and ten pence a pound. This heavy tax might have been expected to discourage smoking and snuffing, but seems, like latter-day tobacco taxes, to have had little effect on consumption.

And it was not only in England that the war against tobacco was being waged. In Russia Tsar Michael decreed in 1634 that anyone found guilty a second time of taking snuff would have his nose amputated. Meanwhile in France Louis XIII tried abolition. Tobacco could only be purchased there by order of a physician, but the French continued to get their tobacco from somewhere, and by the middle of the seventeenth century in France, snuffing

23

was well established. Jean-Baptiste Lully even wrote a trio in its honour, a snuff-taker's canzonetta.

Louis XIV, like his predecessor, was a dedicated anti-snuffer and ordered Fagon, his physician, to address his court on the evil consequences that snuffers were likely to suffer. In 1635, Pope Urban VIII issued a bull excommunicating anyone who took snuff in church, describing it as "an abomination in the sight of God that the clergy take snuff at ecclesiastical councils". But history reveals how seldom it has been possible to damn the flood of fashion. And so it was with the snuffing habit. Church and State thundered and threatened and taxed in vain. Men and women went on snuffing, and the habit swept through Spain, Italy and France in the early years of the seventeenth century, and as the century progressed it became increasingly practised in Holland, Germany, Denmark and Sweden.

Towards the end of the seventeenth century a dramatic change occurred. What until then had been a habit, good or bad depending how you looked at it, suddenly became something quite different. Snuffing developed into an important social grace, and almost into an art form, to which the French gave the name *L'exercice de la tabatière*. As Henri d'Allemagne was to point out, you could now tell much about a man's breeding from the way he took snuff. For a gentleman of fashion snuffing had become a little ballet of the hands. It began with a flourish as the box was produced. Then fingers were tapped on the exquisite little lid as though to gain admittance This knocked the tobacco away from the box opening. Then there was the taking of a pinch of powder with finger and thumb and the carrying of it to the nostrils, the delicate sniff itself, and finally there was a pirouette with the handkerchief to wipe away any offending grains.

The snuffer now lingered long in the shop of his supplier, choosing blends for morning, noon and night, the constituents of which came from the corners of the earth. He chose his snuff with the same consideration that the connoisseur today selects his wines, and he had almost as many possibilities to choose from. Sacheverell Sitwell became so fascinated by the varieties of snuff available to the eighteenth-century customer that he compiled what he called "a geography of snuff". He listed "early sorts, which in their time became old fashioned". These included

24

"Bergamota, Jessamina, Orangely, and Neroly named for the scents from which they were compounded . . ." Then there were

> plain and scented Saint Domingo; Dutch and Strasbourg; Hoxton, and all other sorts of rappee; Spanish, Seville and Havannah, Brazil, Portugal and Bergamot. Others were Macauba, highly scented from Martinique; Princeza from Lisbon; Cuba; Latakia, made from the light tobacco of Persia; Masulipatam, dark, moist, richly scented, brought from the coast of Coromandel; Natchitoches, from Louisiana . . . and Penalvar, a mixture of tobacco and red earth, coming from Havannah, of great pungency and used, also, as a dentifrice.[1]

And there were many more besides these.

Snuffing continued to have its critics. Furetière in 1727 derided those who kept stuffing it into their noses under the misguided belief that it cleared their brains. Everybody, he lamented, was partaking of it, even women and girls. There was, he thought, "something disgusting in seeing the nose of a woman or a girl all smeared with snuff'. But there were many more addicts than there were critics. In the London coffee houses there were "assemblies of snuffing Peripateticks" and Ned Ward wrote of the "clashing of their snuff-box lids in opening and shuting . . ." Kings and queens and their courtiers now embraced the fad as wholeheartedly as once they had inveigled against it, and they often spent fortunes on snuff.

With Louis XIV dead, a new age of indulgence swept France, first under the Regent Philippe d'Orléans, then under Louis XV. So important a part did snuff play in this new age of elegance, that the period has been called the *Siècle de la Tabatière*. Nor was this courtly craze restricted to France. In courts all over Europe they were snuffing, in Catherine the Great's St Petersburg and Frederick the Great's Berlin. In England Queen Anne became an addict and Beau Nash in Bath was for ever snuffing and waving one of those printed handkerchiefs, made especially in dun colours for those who took snuff. Dr Johnson carried his snuff loose in his pockets, and having given up smoking tobacco in favour of snuff, he described smoking as "a shocking thing,

[1] Sitwell, *op. cit.*

25

blowing smoke out of our mouths into other people's mouth, eyes and noses . . ." Queen Charlotte was such an addict that she became known as Snuffy Charlotte. And Lord Petersham, Disraeli's Lord Fitzbooby, left 2,000 lbs of snuff in the room he had set aside at Harrington House for storing it and for the daily ritual of filling his snuff boxes.

Lord Petersham was a customer of Fribourg and Treyer in the Haymarket. This firm which had been started in 1720 by Peter Fribourg, who was probably a Swiss, still continues to sell snuff today from the same bow-fronted Georgian premises where in 1764 the Duke of Bolton, Lord Ancram, Lord Clifford, Lord Halifax, Lord Malpas, Lord Percival, Lord Spencer, Lord Widdrington, Lord Newnham, Lord George Beauclerck, the Duchess of Grafton, Lady Suffolk, Lady Shrewsbury and Mrs Cholmondeley were among their distinguished customers. The firm also had between 1800 and 1836 three kings, a queen, a prince and two princesses on their books.

George IV first became a customer of the firm when he was Prince of Wales. Eventually he had his own special snuff blended for him, King's Morning Mixture, King's Evening Mixture, King's Plain and King's Carotte. But his collection was not restricted to these personal blends. When he died Lord Petersham bought some of his stock, including 18 lbs of Old Bureau, 18 lbs of Old Cologne, 18 lbs of Old Arras and 12 lbs of Old Havre. George Evans, who wrote a history of this firm of which his family had gained control, lists 50 different snuffs which stood in the glass jars on the shelves of the shop in the Haymarket at the sign of the Rasp and Crown, at the beginning of the nineteenth century. And he makes the point that these were just some of the snuffs available at this period. As to the consumption of snuff he writes that

> it is difficult to give an exact idea of the amount of snuff used individually daily. The amount purchased is no guide, for the waste was great . . . Half an ounce per day for individual use would possibly be a very moderate allowance and below average[1]

[1] Evans, George, *The Old Snuff House of Fribourg and Treyer,* privately printed, 1920.

By the time George IV died, the snuff-taking habit was already beginning to fall from general favour, and by 1850 it could no longer be described as a fashionable pursuit in England. Though, of course, many people went on using snuff and still continue to do so. Fribourg and Treyer still sell a great deal of snuff, and any morning in Exmouth Market in Islington one can still see at a tobacconist's shop there the owner weighing out snuff from stoneware jars, and in his showcase there are snuffs with names dating back to the early years of the eighteenth century. The neat birchwood snuff boxes from Russia which he sells to his customers are, however, a far cry from those which were made in their thousands by the eighteenth-century goldsmiths at the height of the *Siècle de la Tabatière*. Sacheverell Sitwell has rated eighteenth-century snuff boxes "among the most lovely and entrancing objects made by human hands".[1] No one viewing the Wrightsman collection in the Jewel Room at the Victoria and Albert Museum, or the great collection in the Louvre in Paris, would accuse Mr Sitwell of hyperbole. It is to the containers made to hold snuff—magnificent containers and humble ones—that we now turn our attention.

[1] Sitwell, *op. cit.*

CHAPTER TWO

EARLY SNUFF CONTAINERS

Shakespeare's certain lord ". . . perfumed like a milliner", held a pouncet box "twixt his finger and thumb", and

> He gave his Nose, and took't away again;
> Who therewith angry, when it next came there,
> Took it in snuff . . .

And then there was that gallant described by Dekker eleven years later in 1609, who "must draw out his tobacco-box, the ladle for the cold snuff into his nostril". On the basis of other rather fragmentary evidence one would imagine that what Hotspur described in *Henry IV Part I,* and what Dekker referred to in *The Gulls Horne-booke,* was a fairly familiar sight in the London of the late sixteenth and early seventeenth centuries—a man of fashion as well as "people of the more ordinary sort" taking snuff from their snuff boxes.

What sort of snuff was taken at this period we do not know. It has been suggested it may not have been tobacco snuff but some aromatic powder taken as a defence against the odorous and noxious airs of London. Nor do we know much about the boxes the Elizabethans took their snuff from. It has been suggested that the man in the street probably used a simple box of pewter, lateen, or horn. The box that a lord or a gallant might have flourished was unlikely at this time to have been simple. Simplicity was not much in evidence in fashionable circles during the reign of Elizabeth I. But nobody knows with any certainty just what they looked like, for not a single Elizabethan snuff box has survived.

It is interesting in fact, that Shakespeare's lord should have adapted a box made for another purpose. He used his pouncet or poncet box, possibly a golden one, as a snuff box. Perhaps then the Elizabethan gold and silversmiths just hadn't got around to devising a purpose-built snuff box by 1598. "Perhaps" is all one can say, for so far as this period is concerned all one can do is to speculate on insufficient evidence, and indeed in compiling a history of snuff boxes one remains in the realms of speculation until quite late in the seventeenth century.

No English gold snuff box made earlier than the end of the seventeenth century has survived. There are supposed to be one or two silver boxes dating back to the Commonwealth period still in existence, but I know of no one who has actually seen one. Restoration silver boxes do exist in considerable numbers. But one wonders how many of these are actually snuff boxes, for there is often considerable difficulty in deciding whether a box was designed for snuff or not.

The size of a box is not a certain indication. Among well authenticated examples of snuff boxes there is everything from the giant to the pigmy. The absence of a hinge on a box does, however, make it unlikely that it was intended to be a portable snuff box. To take snuff from a two-part box while standing at some elegant assembly would have been a conjuring trick hardly to have been accomplished with a good grace. But there is still the possibility that a two-part box of adequate size might be a table snuff box, designed to be used in the home, in a tavern, or, at a later date, in a coffee house. Equally well, of course, such a box could have been a table box intended for smoking tobacco and most of the large two-part boxes of the later seventeenth century are usually described as "tobacco boxes".

Often the attribution of an old box is a matter of opinion, and some museum curators refuse to stick their necks out and ticket their exhibits only as "boxes". This is not unreasonable caution, for the smallworkers of the past made boxes for many purposes. They produced patch boxes to hold the gummed taffeta shapes that women placed on face and bosom to heighten their charms or to hide unsightly pimples. They made suçades, later called bonbonnières, to hold sweetmeats to *se fortifier l'estomac* between meals. They produced little boxes to hold soap, to contain a sponge or toothpicks, and later they made the little vignettes, with their pierced inner lids, which served the same purpose as the Elizabethan pomanders. They were filled with aromatic vinegars,

29

concoctions of nutmeg, cloves and cinnamon or of wormwood and rue, angelica and camphor, scented with rose water or the juice of a lemon. And many beautiful boxes were made with no special purpose in mind, *objets d'art* which made ideal gifts in which the recipient could keep small valuables or treasured mementoes.

The earliest English silver tobacco, or snuff, box of which there is a definite record would seem to be the one that Jackson included in his *Illustrated History of English Plate*[1]. This was made in 1655. It is oval and has the domed lid which was a characteristic feature of the late Caroline boxes, and like many of these, too, it has a coat of arms incised into the lid.

A number of silver boxes survive from the Charles II period, enough to suggest that the body of the typical Charles II tobacco or snuff box was, like the contemporary watch case, a shallow basin with bowed sides. The only difference was that while the watch case was round, the box body was usually oval. This hollow container was raised from flat sheet with a hammer. The silversmith would have had to cut an oval of silver sheet and place it over a depression in the top of one of those lengths of tree trunk which craftsmen even today continue to use for the purpose. He would then have hammered round and round in courses until he had saucered his oval. Having annealed the metal to restore its malleability he would next have placed his saucer against a tee-shaped iron raising stake and with hundreds of deft and deafening blows of the hammer he would have pushed the metal into its final form. With a round-faced planishing hammer he would then have hammered out the ugly marks left by the raising hammer replacing them with a patina of neat hammer marks. At the end of a hard day's work he would have his oval box body completed, all but for the polishing. The typical domed lid of the period would also have been given its form over the depression in the tree trunk, and this having been planished in its turn and polished, it would have gone to the engraver, who with rapid strokes of his sharp graving tool would have cut a coat of arms into the lid, and enclosed the arms within flowing plumes. Sometimes, indeed more often than not, the skills of a chaser rather than an engraver were called upon. In this case, the arms and its encircling feathers

[1] Batsford, B. J., and Jackson, *An Illustrated History of English Plate*, Country Life, 1911.

would have been ponderously delineated a fraction of an inch at a time, for the chaser makes his lines with a tiny chisel struck by a hammer. The silver is pushed aside, and a little furrow is formed in the surface. Another blow and the furrow is lengthened, then another blow, and another and another, and the line gradually grows longer. And each blow must have the same weight or the line will not be even. A good chaser will, however, give greater interest to his design by varying the strengths of the different lines that compose it. It remained now for the smith to solder the two halves of the bold hinge, if the box was provided with one, to the body and lid, and then to drive a silver wire through the lugs of this hinge to make the two halves of the box one.

Most of the few surviving Caroline hinged oval boxes, which were incidentally quite large, being three to four inches across, were fitted with a spring fastening operated by a button on the lid. A typical box of this type is to be seen in the collection at the Victoria and Albert Museum in London.

There are exceptions to every generalisation in the collector's world. Not every Caroline hinged box was oval. Not every box from this period was a plain one, decorated with no more than a coat of arms or a monogram. There is in the Victoria and Albert Museum for example an oblong box with canted corners, the top and side panels of which are decorated all over with chinoiseries in high relief against a matted ground. These panels would seem to have been cast and then the design brightened up by a chaser. The oblong form of this box, which was a gift from Charles II to "Mrs Gwin", was not an uncommon one at the period. Such boxes were included in those elaborate toilet sets of the time. And these sets were also often decorated with either chased or engraved chinoiseries. This is, however, the only snuff box of this type which is known to have survived.

From the end of the seventeenth century we have inherited a number of more decorative silver boxes. One of these made by Benjamin Pine about 1695, is illustrated by Eric Delieb in *Investing in Silver*.[1] This is interesting because it once again reveals close links between watch cases and snuff boxes, and it is by no means unlikely that the same workshops produced both of these. This box has a repoussé plaque on the lid depicting a naked

[1] Delieb, Eric, *Investing in Silver*, Barrie and Rockliff, 1967.

woman nursing a baby with naked children in the background picking flowers, and is supposed to represent the Holy Family. Religious and classical scenes were the favourite motifs of the late seventeenth and early eighteenth centuries and such motifs are often found on watch cases.

EARLY CONTINENTAL BOXES

Continental gold or silver snuff boxes that can be attributed to a date earlier than 1700 are surprisingly rare. One might have expected Spain, as the chief supplier of snuff to Europe in those early days, to have a wealth of them in her museums and private collections. Clare le Corbeiller, however, came to the conclusion that in Spain 'the production of boxes in any material appears to have been wholly insignificant",[1] while Kenneth Snowman wrote of Spain and Portugal producing gold boxes in small quantities, but those he had examined, he said, "exhibit nothing indigenous to their country of origin".[2] My own exhaustive enquiries and researches for early Iberian snuff boxes have proved fruitless and served only to confirm the conclusions of these two writers.

Italy, which was perhaps the first country after Spain where snuff-taking became generally fashionable, is a slightly more rewarding hunting ground. We know from Francesco Zucchi's *La Tabaccheide* that the Italian goldsmiths were making snuff boxes as early as 1636, but I have seen no example of Italian work earlier than the last quarter of the seventeenth century. At this time the goldsmiths were producing gold and silver boxes in the same bombé oval form that was favoured by the English makers. However, the Italian boxes were, as one might expect, a great deal more ebullient. There are a number of Italian silver boxes dating from the late seventeenth century in the Victoria and Albert Museum which are typical (see B/W plate 2). All of them are over-decorated with late Renaissance imagery—scrolls everywhere, acanthus in profusion and the trophies of war in abundance.

Very few early French boxes have survived. The regal disapproval of Louis XIV may have a lot to do with this. To carry a snuff box at Versailles would have been to have courted royal

[1] le Corbeiller, *op. cit.*
[2] Snowman, Kenneth, *Eighteenth-Century Gold Boxes of Europe,* Faber and Faber, 1966.

32

1. Six eighteenth-century French gold snuff boxes from the Ortiz-Patino collection. Top: Enamelled box made in Paris in 1747 by an unidentified maker. Right above: Fine oval box by one of the best Paris makers, Noël Hardivilliers in 1753. The chinese musicians among palm trees are in *basse-taille* enamel (3 details of this box are supplied in plate 2). Left above: Typical deep oval box of the Louis Seize style made by Jean-Baptiste Godart in Paris in 1769. Right below: Painted enamel box with scenes after Teniers by Jean-Marie Tiron, hallmarked in 1755 and 1756. Left below: Box with applied tinted shell decoration against an engraved background. Made by Jean Gaillard in 1746. Bottom: Round box with painted enamels of pet dogs and cats by Francois-Nicolas Génard, Paris 1763 (5 details of this box are supplied in plate 11). Christie's.

2. Three views of a beautiful oval
featuring chinese musicians am
palm trees in *basse-taille* enamel made
Noël Hardivilliers. Paris 1753. Christ

3. Five gold snuff boxes and a sc
bottle in a style sometimes used by
snuff box makers. Top: The mon
bottle was carved from agate in ab
1750. Boxes of this type of English m
exist, but the carved stone was proba
imported and the mounts added
England. Left above: A fine example
relief *basse-taille* type enamel w
against an engraved background. M
in Paris by Jacques-Malquis Le Quir
1749. Right above: Two outstand
French artists combined their talents
produce this box in 1757. The l
itself is the work of the goldsmith Je
François Garand and the enamel pai
ing is by Charles-Jacques de Mai
Left below: The box believed to h
been given by Catherine the Great
Count Stroganoff. Made in gold a
decorated with niello work aga
rayed backgrounds, probably in
Petersburg about 1760. Right belo
Gold box decorated with appl
mother of pearl against engravi
Made by Pierre Aymé Joubert in P
in 1744. Bottom: Pretty oval enamel
box of 1764. Christie's.

4. Enamelled gold box made by Pierre Théremin, the St. Petersburg goldsmith in 1800. Christie's.

5. Oblong transfer-printed and painted early Birmingham snuff box, decorated with an Italianate harbour scene, the side with summer flowers.

6. *Zellenmosaik* box by the Dresden maker Johann Christian Neuber. The central medallion is of lapis lazuli, the other stones are chalcedonies. Christie's.

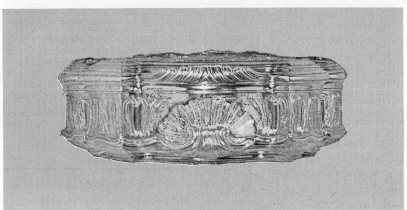

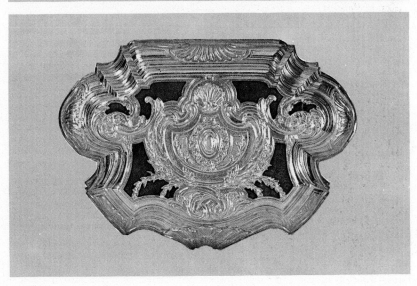

7. Highly important Louis XV royal chased gold and Lapis-Lazuli snuff box, by Juste-Aurèle Meissonnier. Paris 1728. Ortiz-Patino collection. Christie's.

8. A circular gold and enamelled snuff box made by Louis Mailly in Paris between 1720 and 1726. The enamel painting after Watteau on the lid is probably by Jean-Baptiste Massé who owned the original painting by Watteau, called La Finette, at this time. Inside the lid of this little 2½in diameter box is an enamel painting after Lancret. Courtesy Kenneth Snowman.

9. One of the diplomatic boxes made for Frederick the Great probably by the English-born maker John William George Krüger. The box is made of a composition resembling stone and set with foiled diamonds. Courtesy Kenneth Snowman.

10. Six gold boxes made in Paris in the eighteenth century, from the Ortiz-Patino collection. Top: Box decorated with mother-of-pearl made by Jean Gaillard in 1745. Above left: Box made in 1763 by Ambroise-Nicolas Cousinet enamelled *en plein* with Turkish scenes and musical trophies. Above right: Enamel box of about 1787 with panels enamelled *en grisaille*. Bellw left: Box enamelled *en plein* and *en basse taille*. Made in 1750, possibly by Jean-Charles Ducrollay. Below right: *En cage* box with Sevres porcelain panels made by Pierre Croissant in 1744. Bottom: A box from the early 1750's enamelled *en plein* between chased gold chevrons. Christie's.

11. Five views of an oval gold snuff box with painted enamels of pet dogs and cats, by Francois-Nicolas Génard. Paris 1763. Christie's.

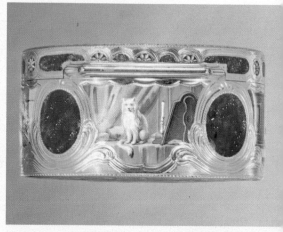

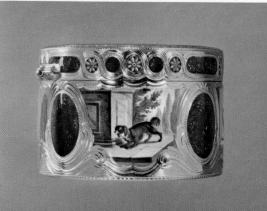

displeasure. But of course to have upon one's person one of the fashionable *boîte-à-portrait* would have been quite acceptable. These shallow boxes, the lids of which bore miniature paintings, were designed to contain a lock of a lady's hair, or an apt couplet perhaps. Then someone got the idea that they might be put to another use. So the Sun King was beguiled, and the *tabatière-à-portrait* was born.

A delightful style of box was produced in France, and in Holland too, in the middle years of the seventeenth century, but whether these pretty boxes were ever used for snuff is not known. This was the age of flowers, of tulipamania and *cosse de pois*, and a number of enchanting watch cases were produced at this time with enamel flower patterns painted all over either on a black or white background. Sometimes floral motifs were applied to the case and enamelled, so giving a high relief effect. The "snuff-boxes", if this is what they were (one of which, probably a Dutch one, is in the collection of Viscount Bearstead), are of exactly the same shape as the watch cases and decorated in just the same ways. The only difference was that the watch cases were fitted with a pendant from which they were hung.

The production of snuff boxes in Scandinavia almost certainly did not start before the eighteenth century. We know, however, that snuff boxes were being produced in Germany as early as 1602, for Heinrich Ulrich engraved some designs for lids in Nuremberg at that time. There were grotesques made in the Italian manner, clearly the ancestors of those Italian boxes from the end of the century. But here as elsewhere the upheavals of wars, the decrees of fashion and the financial ups and downs of individuals have robbed us of more substantial evidence. The convertibility of precious objects mitigates against their survival. At the end of the eighteenth century the Sardinian Ambassador to the French Court sold back to the supplier the box he had received as a gift from the French king. In fact he raised 25,000 livres on it on three separate occasions. He was probably by no means the first man of fashion to pawn his snuff box when pressed by his creditors, and others would not have been so lucky as to have the means to later recoup their pawn.

ENGLISH HORN BOXES

Horn seems to have been used from an early date for snuff boxes, though few examples have survived which can be dated earlier than late seventeenth century. The horner's craft was an ancient one in England. In the fifteenth century the London horners had been expelled from the city and forced to congregate in Petticoat Lane because of the annoyance their stinking trade had caused their neighbours. By the end of the seventeenth century these Petticoat Lane horners were processing the horns of no fewer than 350,000 animals a year.

These horners made boxes by boiling the horn until it was soft, and then pressing it between slabs of iron to produce plates. These plates could be moulded to form oval box bodies, or cut up and welded into oblong receptacles. The fact that horn could be rendered malleable by boiling was also exploited to produce integral decoration, which was pressed into the material from metal dies. Among the Huguenot refugees who fled from France after the revocation of the Edict of Nantes in 1685, were a family of ivory carvers from Dieppe. One of the sons of this family, John Obrisset, adopted the horner's craft and raised the craft of horn moulding to new heights, using the skill in carving which he had inherited from his family to produce dies of very high quality. He worked in London from 1691 to 1728, and is nowadays seen as one of the outstanding craftsmen of the early eighteenth century.

Obrisset's best known pieces are his commemorative snuff boxes, and the finest of these were perhaps his "Drake" boxes. One of these is in the London Museum collection (B/W plate 3), and has the arms of the admiral with a little ship in full sail above them, delicately embossed upon the lid. Though these boxes have sometimes been offered for sale as Elizabethan work, they are usually, in fact, signed and dated. The one in the London Museum is signed in full "John Obrisset 1712". Others just bear the maker's initials.

Other souvenir boxes of this type, made by Obrisset, had pressed onto their flat lids representations of Charles I in armour, a bust of Queen Anne and equestrian portraits of George I and George II. Silver mounts appeared on his later boxes, and to some of these he imparted repoussé silver portraits similar in design to

34

contemporary medals and coins. He also produced some horn boxes with biblical motifs.

Lacking the artistic talents and craftsmanship of Obrisset, other horners decorated their boxes in less sophisticated ways. They rendered them silky-black in colour with silver nitrate or tinted them with dyes, decorated them with gilding, or set the lid with a central stone or a carved ivory medallion.

In the second half of the eighteenth century cheap horn boxes were produced by dissolving fragments of horn to form a paste which was then moulded to form base and lid.

TORTOISE-SHELL BOXES

An even better organic substance than horn was used for making snuff boxes from the late seventeenth century onwards. This was the substance which has always been known as tortoise-shell, though it should more properly be called turtle-shell, for the best material has always been sliced from the carapace of the hawksbill turtle.

Like horn this shell could be softened in boiling water and moulded, and designs could be pressed into it. A favourite form of decoration was to mould fluting on the body and lid, and in the centre of the lid where the rays of the fluting met, a silver ornament was usually applied. Obrisset, who worked in tortoise-shell as well as in horn and produced a series of moulded royal portrait boxes, also applied portraits in silver to a number of fluted boxes, notably one with a double portrait of Prince George of Denmark and Queen Anne, an example of which can be seen in the British Museum in London.

Many of the tortoise-shell boxes made in Europe during the two-hundred-year period from the middle of the seventeenth century to the middle of the nineteenth were decorated with piqué work. Piqué work consisted of a design in gold or silver inserted into the surface of an organic material, usually tortoise-shell, but sometimes ivory too. Three different types of piqué work are differentiated. There is *point piqué*, or *piqué d'or*, which consists of a pattern of tiny gold or silver pins inserted into the surface. Sometimes, usually when the pattern is an intricate one, this type of piqué is also known as *foulé point d'or*. When large pins are used instead of the tiny ones this is known as stud or nail

35

piqué or *clouté d'or*. Thirdly there is that piqué which consists of strips of gold or silver inserted into the shell. To elaborate the pattern, the strips were sometimes chased or engraved. This is known as *piqué posé*. Sometimes more than one form of piqué will appear on the same snuff box. *Clouté d'or* are sometimes mixed in with *piqué d'or*. Like accented notes in a piece of music they bring rhythm and order to the composition. Then when *point piqué* is used with *piqué posé* work it has the effect of giving it an appearance of delicacy it would not otherwise have had.

Piqué work may originally have been devised in Italy, but it was in France that it became a minor art form in the second half of the seventeenth century. A form of piqué work was also being used by English tortoise-shell workers from the reign of Charles II, but this was quite different from that on continental boxes from this period, consisting of little gold circles, usually placed in tiny pyramids round the edge of the lid of the oval boxes. This motif was incidentally first found on goldwares from the Minoan/Mycenaean period. Occasionally these circles are formed into radiating lines as on the fluted lid of a box which bears an applied head of Charles II. Incidentally, this box bears a marked resemblance to some of the memento boxes of Obrisset and was, I believe, probably made in the early eighteenth century, though Herbert C. Dent in his monograph on piqué work attributes it to the Caroline period. On some boxes the little circles form monograms, and on others they accompany little flower and bird motifs in *piqué posé* work.[1]

The French piqué work from the Louis XIV period is much more sophisticated than the English. The earliest pieces are usually decorated with a mixture of very delicate *point piqué* interspersed with *nail piqué*. The motifs consist of monograms, fans, lattices, baroque architectural details, insects, trailing vines and imagery with royal association like the sun and the peacock—the sun bird. These are usually surrounded by a frame consisting of the "C" scrolls which were so much a feature of baroque decoration. The boxes to which this decoration is applied are usually oval, but occasionally oblong. Later Louis XIV boxes were more often than not oblong, and these were usually decorated with a mixture of *piqué posé* and *point piqué*.

[1] Dent, Herbert C., *Piqué, A Beautiful Minor Art*, London, 1923.

36

At the beginning of the eighteenth century the effects of the revocation of the Edict of Nantes resulted in the spread of French culture throughout Europe, and it is probable that boxes in the French style, believed to have been produced in Germany and Holland at this time were the work of refugee French piqué workers. It must be said, however, that the attribution of these boxes to a particular country of origin is difficult if not impossible.

Among the 4,000 Huguenot families who settled in England in the late seventeenth century, it seems likely that there were some piqué artists who decorated snuff boxes for English customers, which would explain the existence of English boxes decorated in the French style at this period.

By the first decade of the eighteenth century the English tortoise-shell workers were, however, beginning to favour quite a different type of decoration, consisting of *piqué posé* work combined with mother of pearl appliqué. The presence in some of these designs of unmistakably Dutch figures has led to the suggestion that they were the work of Dutch artists who had accompanied William III when he came over with Mary to replace James II on the English throne.

From the early eighteenth century onwards most English piqué work was *piqué posé* work, and hardly ever is any *point piqué* present. What must be the finest example of a *piqué posé* English box is the large baroque-shaped table box in the Jones Collection, now in the Victoria and Albert Museum. The piqué work, which depicts the Roman goddess of war, Bellona, showing the plans of a fortification to a general, is repousséd and clearly the work of a very fine chaser.

In France too from the 1720s *piqué posé* became popular, but the designs are often elaborated with point detail, and there was a revival there of point work in the 1750s when Jean George among others employed it to create work of unsurpassed delicacy.

During the reign of Louis XVI a new type of *point piqué* came into fashion, the points taking the form of stars rather than dots, and the design often consisting of no more than a patina of bright stars on the glossy surfaces of the tortoise-shell. Later still little floral motifs were scattered over the surfaces, or bands and borders of the most delicate *piqué posé* work were inserted in the shell.

In the second half of the eighteenth century, in what furniture historians call the Chippendale period, the English tortoise-shell boxmakers employed somewhat ugly *piqué posé* work derived from furniture motifs. This was followed by a period when the piqué workers used mounts in the Adam style on their oval- and shuttle-shaped boxes, stylised honeysuckle and pendant husks, festoons and fans. This in turn gave place to Hepplewhite decoration. The boxes of this period were invariably shuttle-shaped, usually with a central oval medallion, either a painting or an engraved metal plaque, but sometimes a spray of flowers of chased *piqué posé* work. The lids had edge decoration usually in the form of a twisted rope design, but sometimes they had leaf and flower garlands round the rim of the lid.

Ivory boxes as has been said were sometimes decorated with piqué work throughout this period, the types of decoration on early English boxes was of the ring type and later *piqué posé* came into fashion. Surviving ivory boxes decorated with piqué are, however, comparatively rare, perhaps because this form of decoration was much less effective against the yellow/white background than against the shiny brown surface of tortoise-shell.

Though piqué work was produced over a period of two centuries, it was a seventeenth-century invention and the most charming examples, with a few notable exceptions, came from the late seventeenth and early eighteenth-century period.

It is very difficult to date any of the boxes made from organic materials, because even when heavy gold or silver mounts or inlays were used these were never hallmarked. It has been asserted that the mounts and inlays on English boxes made between 1697 and 1720 would probably have been of the higher Britannia Standard. All forms of assaying are more or less destructive, however, and unless a box was already much marred, it is unlikely that anyone would sacrifice condition in search of truth. So in most instances style is the only guide, and the dating of minor works of art on the basis of style alone is fraught with uncertainties.

FLASKS, HORNS AND RASPS

Apart from boxes there were two other types of receptacles for holding powdered tobacco in use from the middle of the seventeenth century. These were the snuff flask and the snuff horn (see B/W plate 4). A good number of snuffers at one time also rasped their own snuff.

There is in the Wallace Collection in London a rare example of an early English snuff flask—what the French called a *poire-à-poudre*. This flask resembles the powder flasks which soldiers carried, but lacks the nozzle usual on these. It is the more interesting, this flask, because it has royal connections. It is covered with black shagreen, and this is decorated with gold piqué, the dots forming on one side a star and garter, and on the other the monogram of Charles II below a crown. The gold mount at the mouth is a rather complicated castor top, which allowed just the right amount of snuff to be shaken on to the hand. There is a very odd reference in the Memoirs of Thomas Bruce, second Earl of Ailesbury, to Charles II ordering "one to be made which he wore with a string on his wrist and did not open, but the snuff came out by shaking". The reason why Charles ordered this container was, it would seem, because he got fed up with the Duke of Lauderdale "continually putting his fingers into the King's snuff box. . . ." One wonders if Charles had seen such containers on his travels before his restoration. Snuff flasks were already common in Scandinavia, where they date back to 1600 or earlier, and they existed in Germany too. There is, incidentally, also a flask, of similar form to the Charles II one, in the Victoria and Albert Museum collection, but this is made of tortoise-shell mounted in silver. It is decorated in *point piqué* with representations of a dog, a stag and a tree. The style of the piqué work suggests that this is French and it was probably made in the last quarter of the seventeenth century.

The earliest surviving examples of Scandinavian flasks date from the 1650s and 1660s. A Finnish horn snuff flask of purse form, with engraved bands, and inscribed with the date 1669, is to be seen in the National Museum in Helsinki. The more usual Finnish snuff container was, however, the snuff horn, early examples of which can also be seen in the National Museum. These were in the form of flattened animal horns, the broad end of which was closed, often with a silver mount, and the narrow end was fitted with a nozzle. The user placed the nozzle to his nose and shook in the snuff. In fact in Finland, where snuffing is still as popular as it ever was, these horns continue to be preferred by many people to boxes, and are still being produced there.

There survive in Norway a number of silver-mounted wooden snuff flasks made in the late seventeenth century and throughout the eighteenth. Most of these are in the form of flat-sided bottles, the same shape, that is, as the snuff bottles which the Chinese later made in glass or carved from gem material. The Norwegian flasks were carved out of wood, and decorative silver mounts were pinned on to the top and bottom of the vessel, while a central silver plaque on the side was also a common feature. The style of these chased silver mounts is often useful in dating them. Little dumpy and rotund silver-mounted flasks also survive and, judging from the style of the mounts, these may well have been the earlier type of Norwegian snuff container.

Similar flasks in wood, horn and ivory were made in Germany. The German flasks which date from the second half of the seventeenth century were highly decorative as all German applied art was at that time. Some were like the Finnish horns in shape, others like the dumpy Norwegian flasks. The standard of decoration varied considerably. A horn in the Hessisches Landesmuseum at Kassel for instance is a fine example of sophisticated wood-carving in the baroque manner. The carving on some of the little flasks is of that rather inept kind, and might be called village craft baroque. It has little to recommend it except a certain charm acquired by age.

One cannot leave the subject of snuff flasks without mentioning that odd English wooden box illustrated by Eric Delieb in *Investing in Silver*.[1] It looks at first glance like a Finnish wooden flask, but in fact it is a box. The side bears a silver mount engraved "John Dune 1709" and is hinged.

The snuff rasp seems to have been a late seventeenth-century invention, and rasps exist which were made in many European countries. The rasp came into use not because ready-powdered snuff was not easily available, but because so many purveyors were not to be trusted. They couldn't resist the temptation of making a little go a lot further by diluting the tobacco with additives. So people began to buy a "carrot" of tobacco, a roll of compressed tobacco leaves, and to rasp their own snuff. Rasping

[1] Delieb, *op. cit.*

seems to have been practised by the lofty and less elevated alike, to judge from the rasps that have survived, which range from fine silver cased ones to ones in simple wooden boxes. There is a French engraving of about 1700 which shows Monsieur L'Abbé, a man obviously very much *à la mode*, using his rasp. The cover of his rasp, which is hinged, is shown open revealing the steel grater underneath, and he holds a carrot that must be all of nine inches long in his other hand.

The late Edward Pinto's fascinating collection of "Wooden Bygones", much of which is now in the Birmingham Museum and Art Gallery, included rasps with both wood and ivory covers. The ivory ones, which are finely carved with contemporary and classical scenes, are French in origin as probably are those in the Tobacco Museum in Amsterdam. The Pinto collection includes some interesting wooden rasps from Central Europe and Russia, which are either heavily carved or inlaid with mother-of-pearl. The existence of wooden rasps in Germany is vouched for by an example in the collection of the German tobacco firm of Reemtsma, which depicts one man offering rasped snuff to another, and in the Kunstindustrimuseet in Copenhagen there is a Dresden enamel-ware rasp depicting Abraham and Isaac.

Perhaps the most elegant of surviving rasps is one in the Victoria and Albert Museum collection in London. It dates from about 1700, and has that satisfying simplicity of the best Queen Anne silverwares. It is truncheon-shaped with a flat top and base and straight sides. At one end there is a little hinged compartment designed perhaps to hold a small carrot, but more probably to hold the powdered tobacco. The larger hinged lid, which has on it an engraving of a three-masted ship, the arms of Edmund of York, lifts to reveal a steel rasp.

Besides the pocket rasps, ceremonial rasps were produced for passing round a table. These measured from thirty to forty-five centimetres long. There are a number of these in the Pinto collection in the Birmingham Museum. One dated as late seventeenth-century is carved with a representation of Abraham and Isaac and is probably Flemish. Another one, interestingly decorated with a coat of arms outlined in brass piqué, is probably eighteenth-century, as is also another one with a coat of arms on it with a bold shell end, believed to be Austrian. There is also a Dutch ceremonial rasp of 1725 supplied with wheels so that it could be rolled across the table like the silver ship neffs with their cargo of wine.

It seems as though some snuffers still preferred to grate their own snuff from the carrot long after there was any necessity to do so. Snuff rasps dating from the end of the eighteenth century and the beginning of the nineteenth exist. An interesting example of a late date is a little silver urn in the Adam style, made in Germany and now in a Danish private collection. This urn is hinged at the base and opens to reveal the rasp, a rasp much too boldly toothed to have been intended, as most rasps of this period were, for the grating of nutmegs.

PART TWO

CHAPTER ONE

THE GOLDEN AGE OF THE SNUFF BOX
1700 to 1800

Anyone who writes an account of snuffing and the snuff boxes of the sixteenth and the seventeenth centuries is aware of having to make too many educated guesses based on fragmentary evidence. When it comes to the eighteenth century, however, at least from the end of the second decade onwards, one is faced with an embarrassment of riches. Eighteenth-century snuff boxes have survived in their thousands, and there are hundreds of references in the literature of the period, and a wealth of contemporary paintings, drawings and engravings show people from all walks of life indulging in snuff.

That snuffing was a universal habit restricted to no one class was made clear by Hogarth, that relentless commentator on the follies and the evils of his age. On the steps of Gin Lane he placed a raddled and ragged hag, who had fatally relinquished her hold on the baby she was nursing in order to seek the solace of her snuff box. From the other end of the social scale, one of the pictures from the *Mariage à la Mode* series shows the foppish lord taking snuff with a considered flourish. Clearly he was one of those who elegantly "just dip the tip of the middle Finger in the Box", and not one of those less dainty, who took a pinch "bitwixt the Thumb and the fore Finger".

While many an artist and author could not disguise his contempt for, or amusement at, such a foolish affectation, the portrait painters, who were paid to flatter their sitters, often included a snuff box as a symbol of elegance and fashion in their paintings. Colley Cibber, the actor, was painted flourishing his box. Lord Hawkesbury holds one negligently in his hand. French artists portrayed women of fashion in the act of taking snuff. In Denmark and Sweden too, snuff-taking was a favourite subject with both portrait painters and caricaturists.

45

In the eighteenth century the snuff box was the gift for all occasions. In France it was the accepted diplomatic gift as the *Registre des Présents du Roi* reveals. On a private level it was a very acceptable gift of friendship or a plight of love. It could also be a peace offering. Laurence Sterne in his *Sentimental Journey*, having refused an appeal for alms from a Franciscan monk, realised that he had "behaved very ill". Eventually he was able to make amends. On a second meeting the monk

> having a horn snuff-box in his hand, presented it open to me —You shall taste mine—said I, pulling out my box (which was a small tortoise one) and putting it into his hand—'Tis most excellent, said the monk; Then do me the favour, I replied, to accept of the box and all, and when you take a pinch out of it, sometimes recollect it was the peace-offering of a man who once used you unkindly, but not from his heart.

As to the boxes themselves that emerged glittering from the workshops of the eighteenth-century smallworkers, they present a bewildering variety of styles, and were made in every conceivable material, enriched with every form of decoration devised by craftsmen. Many of the boxes are microcosms of the life of the century, detailing the thrill of the chase, the leisured summertime *fête champêtre*, even the pornographic intimacies of the boudoir.

CHAPTER TWO

FRENCH BOXES OF THE EIGHTEENTH CENTURY

Louis XIV's aversion to snuff-taking obviously discouraged the production of fine gold snuff boxes during his reign. As the entire nobility lived at Versailles "couped up in a perpetual house party", snuff-taking had to be indulged in secretly, and snuff boxes had to be discreet rather than showy. The Sumptuary Edict of 1700 was yet a further discouragement. The sumptuary laws of the past, relating to precious metals and jewels, had been designed to restrict these to the royal family and to the establishment. By ancient tradition such things were the prerogative of the nobility, symbols of power and prestige. The Act of 1700 was designed, however, not to bolster aristocratic pride but to conserve the gold stocks of the nation. France was, as she had been on and off for years, bankrupt again. So the Edict was promulgated stipulating that not more than one ounce of gold might be used in the production of a single ware.

Neither the royal displeasure nor this royal Edict were totally effective. The court continued to practise *l'exercice de la tabatière*. It was the fashion, and the flourishing of a delightful little box was an essential part of the proceedings; as important as the snuff-taking itself, and the men and women of fashion had to have their snuff boxes. So sometimes the Edict was ignored, and sometimes the boxmakers of Paris found ways round the law. They devised, for instance, a new style of box, to become famous later in the century as the *en cage* style. The lid, base and walls of these boxes were composed of panels of decorative minerals or of organic materials such as horn, tortoise-shell or mother-of-pearl, these panels being encaged in ornamental gold mounts. But increasingly the fashionable went elsewhere to buy what they were not allowed to buy at home. A thriving import trade in gold boxes grew up and reached such proportions in the last years of

47

the King's reign that it became a drain on the economy and the purpose of the Edict was defeated. It was not until the Regency in 1721 that the amount of gold permitted to be used for one snuff box was at last increased to seven ounces, and native craftsmanship was encouraged to compete with the imports.

Of those boxes that were made despite the law, not a single example of a Louis XIV gold one, that can with certainty be said to be a snuff box, has survived. Indeed few French gold boxes of any kind have come down to us from this or any period earlier than the second decade of the eighteenth century.

Gold artefacts have always been in danger. They have been melted down to fit out an army, or to facilitate the division of the spoils among the victors after a battle. They have gone into the melting pot in their thousands to alleviate private and national disasters. There were many such in the reign of Louis XIV. In 1687 and 1689 the King melted down some of his treasures and called upon his court to follow his example to help support France's tottering economy. Those treasures new and old which escaped these two meltings down were probably sacrificed during the troubled years of 1709 and 1710. At this time, two bad harvests threatened Paris with famine, and whereas in the past on such occasions Louis had been able to distribute "the King's bread" purchased from his private purse, this time he was too poor even to do this. He was at war with the Allies and the war was not going well. The King eventually parted with his gold plate and raised the equivalent of 81,000 livres, and again he called upon his people to follow his example and to part with their treasures to help their country. Many a gold snuff box must have been sacrificed at this time, when soldiers sold their muskets and officers their linen in order to buy bread.

It is for these reasons that we have to rely upon the engravings and drawings that have come down to us, in particular the designs of Claude Bérain, Masson and J. G. Roberday, to give us an idea of what the early eighteenth-century French gold snuff box must have looked like. The designs suggest that the forms of those early boxes were simple. Most of the designs were for oblong boxes, though there are one or two for oval and round ones. If, however, the form was straightforward, the decoration was anything but restrained. The current fashion in all the applied arts was for lavish decoration, and the designers depicted boxes every square centimetre of which was chased in relief. The motifs were complex baroque compositions, many of them derived from the grotesques popular in Italy a century earlier. A typical Bérain design depicted a composition of scrolls, acanthus and shells, while Roberday obviously had a penchant for those coy little apes, dressed in fashionable clothes, desporting among ruins hung with vines heavy with grapes.

The few surviving silver snuff boxes from this period confirm the impression given by the designs. The silver box of 1720, illustrated by Bo Bramsen in *Nordiske Snusdaser*[1] shows that the style persisted for two decades. This oval box with its bold hinge and slightly bowed lid is decorated with chased acanthus scrolls round a decorative central cartouche.

After the death of Louis XIV in 1715, the Regent, the dissipated Philippe d'Orléans, gave great encouragement to the snuff box makers. He was a dedicated snuffer with a taste for luxury. Despite the fact that France was still virtually bankrupt, he indulged his taste without restraint, and among his possessions at the time of his death was a collection of snuff boxes valued at a million livres. He is said to have owned a box for every day of the year, but this rather glib measure of self-indulgence and enthusiasm for the box makers' art was something of a cliché in the eighteenth century. Frederick the Great, Madame de Pompadour and Napoleon were all rumoured to have had a collection of 375 snuff boxes. When Louis XV finally came into his own in 1722, he also proved to be a great patron of the boxmakers. As Nancy Mitford reminds us, he was particularly "fond of little things exquisite in quality".[2]

The boxmakers who supplied the Regent and his court were established on the Quai des Orfèvres and around the Place Dauphine on the Ile de la Cité, just across the Pont Neuf from the great Palais de Louvre. This area today looks singularly decrepit. The goldsmiths have long departed, and its only claims to attention are the famous equestrian statue of Henry IV on the bridge and the offices of the Police Judiciaire. In the eighteenth century, however, the Quai des Orfèvres, named for

[1] Bramsen, Bo, *Nordiske Snusdaser*, Politikensforlag, 1965.
[2] Mitford, Nancy, *The Sun King*, Hamish Hamilton, 1966.

those who practised their craft there, must have rung with the sound of hammers on gold. And from its cramped workshops, lit by the flames from the annealing hearths over which the goldsmiths restored the natural malleability of the metal hardened by their hammering, came during the next eighty years some of the most exquisite creations ever to be devised by mankind.

The makers of these superb boxes were a select and strictly regulated band of craftsmen, supervised by the powerful Guild of Goldsmiths. Unless one were the son of a practising goldsmith, in which case things were a little easier, membership of this tightly knit and highly respected craft was hard to achieve. The would-be goldsmith had first to attain acceptance as an apprentice by a master craftsman and then to work for eight years at his master's bench, slowly learning the skills of the trade. He had then to submit a masterpiece, which he had made with his own hands, to the wardens of the Guild. If they were satisfied that he possessed sufficient skill to uphold the status of the craft, he then had to offer himself for examination by the officials of the Mint. And even if these two bodies were satisfied that he had the necessary ability and integrity he might still be years from achieving his goal. It was a case of waiting for a dead man's shoes, for the number of master goldsmiths allowed to practise their craft at any one time was strictly limited.

When a vacancy did at last occur, then and only then could he strike his maker's mark upon a piece of copper and deposit it at the Mint. This mark, which he must punch into every box he made, consisted of his initials below a crowned *fleur-de-lis*, usually together with his symbol, called his *different*. That great maker Jean George adopted a five-pointed star as his *different*, Louis-Philippe Demay used a tree, and Louis Mailly used a mallet, a pun on his surname. The maker's mark also incorporated two dots, the *grains de remède*, symbolising the degree of tolerance permitted in the purity of the gold the maker submitted to the Mint. He was allowed a tolerance of 0·25 carats below the standard of quality which was 22 carats. That is to say, the gold consisted of 22 parts in 24 of pure gold. The standard was reduced to 20·25 carats between 1721 and 1789. Thereafter small articles were permitted to be made to an even lower standard of 18·25 carats.

Even after a man had become his own master his work and his workshops remained under the surveillance of the wardens of the Guild. His hours of working were laid down, his premises had to be open to inspection and every box he made had to be submitted for testing. After it had passed the assay, the wardens punched a mark into the box which guaranteed the purity of the gold alloy used in its making. The warden's mark for Paris—other towns had their own guilds and their own marks—consisted, up to 1783, of a letter beneath a crown indicating the year of marking. After 1783 all Paris goldwares were marked with the letter P below a crown, and the date was indicated by the last two figures of the year of marking.

Besides these two marks, the maker's mark and the warden's mark, eighteenth-century gold snuff boxes bear two other marks, known as the charge and décharge marks. These were duty marks, a tax being levied on all gold and silver wares.

The duty marks were placed upon the box by the Fermier of the Mint. Succeeding Fermiers had their own personal charge and décharge marks, among which were the heads of birds and animals, a shell, a portcullis and monograms. The maker of a box first submitted it in an unfinished state, and had he done this between 1721 and 1727 the Fermier Charles Cordier would have stamped a charge mark into it representing a hand. When the piece was finally finished, sometimes a year or more later, it was submitted again, and the duty was paid at the current rate when it received the décharge mark. For this Fermier Cordier employed the mark of a bird symbolising the Holy Spirit.

Some of the surviving work of the finest boxmaker of the Regency period, Daniel Gouers, bears the charge and décharge marks of Fermier Cordier. Gouers was a Dutchman who had settled in Paris, and whose name before he gallicised it had been Govaers. He first registered his mark at the Mint in 1717, and he enjoyed a considerable reputation in court circles until 1737. In that year he went bankrupt and fled to Brussels to escape his creditors, taking with him his book-keeper's wife.

Illustrated in B/W plate 6 is a fine example of the work of Daniel Gouers from the Louvre collection. This baroque form box, which was made for Louis XV in 1727, illustrates how box-making in France had become, by the second decade of the eighteenth century, something more than a craft. The gold box had become an art form, and this little work of art had assumed an almost unbelievable importance in fashionable circles. As has already been mentioned, it was said that "a man's background and upbringing were laid bare by the simple art of taking snuff." And just as revealing of a man's taste and position in life, as that little ballet of the fingers which snuff-taking had become, was the box from which he took his snuff. A man like Gouers, who could be depended upon to make something apt for a royal gift or to soften a woman's heart or to politely bribe a man of influence, was continually in demand.

The Gouers box in the Louvre is worth a second look, for not only is it a beautiful work of art, it is also a technical *tour de force*. Boxes like this one justify the vigorous control of the Guild. It is not easy to think of it in terms of skilfully fabricated gold sheet, any more than it is to assess a painting by Watteau in terms of pigment and canvas, yet this Gouers box was the result not just of inspiration but of very considerable skill. The lid, the base and the walls began as an ingot of gold, which had to be hammered and rolled to form a sheet, perfectly flat and polished like a mirror. The various components then had to be formed with the hammer over a swaging block; the lid given its subtly domed form; the complex curves of the walls created. Those perfectly proportioned mounts that delineated the edges of lid and base were made by hammering the gold into channels and the sheet that formed base and lid had to be skilfully bent to produce that perfect piece of miniature engineering which is the hinge. Then these components had to be soldered together so skilfully that the joins were all but invisible, and when all was done the lid must fit the body so perfectly that not one grain of the finely powdered snuff would escape into the owner's pocket. Next the box had to receive its decoration: the delicate courses of flowers, their matted background, the head of Apollo and the sunburst that surrounds it, the little raised mounts that hold the diamonds and emeralds all called for thousands of deftly placed blows with hammer and punches. It seems impossible that this perfect little box, for it measures only 9 cm. by 6·5 cm. by 3 cm., could have been wrought with nothing more sophisticated than hammer, flame and punch by techniques that had been in use for thousands of years.

52

When one opens the lid of this box one finds that it is in fact a *tabatière-à-portrait*, for the distinguished miniaturist Jean-Baptiste Massé had produced a fine painting of the young Louis XV in armour to line the lid. Even in 1727 a king had to pay a king's ransom of 2,100 livres for a box like this.

It is unlikely that this box, even apart from the miniature which Massé contributed, was the work of Gouers alone. When we attribute a box to the man whose mark it bears we are probably doing scant justice to a number of anonymous specialist craftsmen who contributed their skills to its making. We know, for instance, that at the time of his bankruptcy Gouers was making use of a famous member of another guild, Gérard Débêche. Débêche was a graver and chiseller and Gouers had deposited two boxes with him, presumably so that he might carry out chasing upon them. It would have been uncommon for the man who formed a box to also have decorated it, but except in the case of Débêche, the names of the chasers and engravers who added so much to the eighteenth-century French snuff boxes have not come down to us.

If one looks at the public and private collections of these beautiful boxes, one becomes aware of how many different specialists there must have been in Paris contributing to the making of them. There were the enamellers, of course, and different enamellers probably had their own specialities. Some of them would have been specialists in painting *en plein*—painting scenes and motifs direct on to the gold sheet. Others would have produced the *basse-taille* enamelling, a subtler form of the *champlevé* technique which had been used for the decoration of gold wares for thousands of years. These *basse-taille* enamellers scooped out areas of the gold with a graver, varying the depth of the cut so that when they filled the recesses with translucent enamel the shade of the enamel varied depending upon its thickness.

Besides the enamellers there were also those artists and craftsmen who produced the panels for the *en cage* boxes. Among these were the tortoise-shell workers, and those who decorated this glossy shell with pique work. There were the artists who created complex chinoiserie by applying chips of tinted shell to sheets of mother-of-pearl. There were the lapidaries who polished the panels of agate with their eye-like bandings, and those glyptic workers who carved decorative stones. Panels too came from the studios of miniature painters, from the famous ceramic works of Sèvres, and even from the workshops of the painstaking Japanese lacquer artists, and from those like the brothers Martin who produced, with varying degrees of success, substitutes for oriental lacquer.

What resulted from the availability of all these specialist skills was infinite variety. What the fashionable snuffer wanted above all else was a box that was different from everyone else's box—one that would, when it was produced, create an effect. It was this continual search on the part of the boxmakers to bring forth the novelty to please their rich and discriminating patrons, which leaves us with such a bewildering heritage. Anyone who visits the collection in the Louvre or in the Jewellery Gallery at the Victoria and Albert Museum for the first time finds themselves confused by an apparent chaos of styles. B/W Plates 7, 8 and 9 show three boxes from the Louvre collection, each chosen to illustrate a different decorative technique. One could easily have shown ten times as many, and still not have exhausted the variations of form, technique and motif employed by these infinitely versatile goldsmiths who worked on the Quai des Orfèvres in the middle years of the eighteenth century.

If one studies these boxes, however, one does begin to discover some order among this chaos. One begins to be able to chart the fashions that came and went, to know from the evidence of form and decoration to which decade a box belongs and even, without reference to the marks, to sense from whose workshop it came.

The fashionable snuff box of the twenties and thirties of the eighteenth century, for example, had a baroque outline like the Gouers box already described. These shaped boxes are given various names. "Bombé form", "shell-shaped", "cartouche" and "bag-shaped" are all terms used to describe the various types, but I think perhaps the term "baroque" is the most convenient label for them. The walls of these baroque boxes were sometimes slightly bulbous, like the contemporary commodes, and the edge of the lid, and sometimes the base as well, was strengthened and decorated by a tiered moulding like an architrave. Most of the boxes from this period were heavily decorated, usually chased all over. Frequently different coloured golds were used to add interest to the design, the box either constructed of sections made from different alloys, or by inlaying one alloy in another. These boxes made from a number of different coloured golds were known as *trois-couleur* or *quatre-couleur*. The coloured alloys used for these boxes were produced by melting the gold with various proportions of other metals. By increasing the copper content of the gold a red tone was produced. A high silver content produced white gold. Blue gold contained iron or arsenic, while green gold resulted from alloying with silver and cadmium.

The chased designs on these baroque boxes usually incorporated architectural motifs. On some boxes classical façades were the sole subject matter, while on others these motifs formed the surrounds and backgrounds for figure groups—the figures sometimes in contemporary costume, sometimes dressed as classical heroes or in the undress of classical deities. In such an individual art as that of the boxmaker there were, however, many exceptions to this fashionable format. Gouers, for example, produced oblong boxes, including a number in the *en cage* style. One box he made in 1725 had panels of mother-of-pearl carved all over with a shell pattern. Another had panels of sardonyx with an applied floral motif set with gemstones.

In the 1720s the rococo style was born, freeing the decorative arts from the perfectly balanced formalities of the baroque, for a characteristic element of the rococo was asymmetry. One of the founders of the rococo was the expatriate Italian decorator and goldsmith, Juste-Aurèle Meissonnier. Meissonnier has left us a number of his designs for rococo snuff box lids, some of which can be seen in the Musée des Arts Décoratis in Paris. Most of these depict variations on an asymmetric shell motif. Only one gold box which can be definitely attributed to Meissonnier survives. This is a box of very complicated form bearing the chased gold arms of the wife of Charles II of Spain over a lapis-lazuli panel, set off-centre between rococo scrolls. Meissonnier, however, influenced many other boxmakers, in Paris and elsewhere in Europe, over the next two decades. Gouers, for instance, came under the spell of the rococo and in 1734 made a delightful box of rococo forms, decorated with chased chinoiseries against the granulated ground for which he seems to have had a penchant.

The form of this unusual box is derived from a shell, and even the lid of it is unevenly bowed, as though its maker was determined to avoid unfashionable straight lines at all costs.

The inevitable reaction to the disorderly forms of the high rococo set in. From the 1740s the majority of boxes produced were of a simple rectangular form. These newly fashionable deep rectangular boxes may have been simple in outline, but their makers lavished upon them every conceivable type of decoration. It was at this period that there was a revival of interest in the various types of enamel decorations that the seventeenth-century watch-case makers had used to such effect. The enamelled boxes produced during the next thirty years, from the workshops of such craftsmen as Noël Hardivilliers, Jean Ducrollay and Jean George, are perhaps the most beautiful of all the products of the boxmaker's art. The technique of decorating goldwares by filling cavities in the metal with powdered glass, mixed with metallic oxides suspended in liquid, and the fusing of this compound in a muffle was a very ancient one. The French boxmakers now raised this ancient art to new heights. Look, for example, at the box now in the Jewellery Gallery in the Victoria and Albert Museum which came from the workshops of Michel-Robert Hallé about 1750 (B/W plate 10), and see how he has exploited the possibilities of the *basse-taille* technique to produce an exotic and delightful box. He has depicted peacocks and ostriches among trees and flowers using a restricted pallet of blues, greens and reds with white, and has contrasted the sleek surface of the enamel with texturing, the surrounding areas being engraved with an all-over diaper pattern.

Painted enamelling, brought to perfection by Jean Toutin in the seventeenth century, was also now revived. Usually this technique was used to decorate reserved areas, and the technique of applying to these floral bouquets or copies of popular paintings by the French artists Watteau, Lancret, Boucher or of the Flemish artist Teniers, was that described as *en plein* to differentiate it from the technique of mounting painted enamelled panels *en cage*.

The boxes decorated *en plein* often had borders of *basse-taille* enamelling, the boldly coloured floral and foliate sprays and ribbons framing the more subtly coloured central motifs. There are among the boxes in the Louvre many examples decorated with painted enamels *en plein*, but none more delightfully than that made by Barnabé Sagaret, a box surely intended to be used by one of the women of the court who practised *l'exercice de la tabatière* as avidly as the men. This oblong box has bunches of full-blown pink roses depicted upon all its surfaces, perfectly composed in lively and subtle hues. Radiating from these freshly gathered roses are sunbursts, the bright rays deeply scored into the metal, and each panel is framed with boldly chased rococo borders. Did ever goldsmith, chaser, engraver and enameller combine their talents to better effect than they did to produce this little 7·5 cm.-long box, upon which Fermier of the Mint, Julien Berthe, placed his cow's head charge mark in 1754 and his hen's head décharge mark the following year?

Another fine oblong box in the Louvre collection is one by Jacques-Malquis le Quin, which illustrates an intriguing type of decoration. The colourful birds and the green foliage that decorate the lid and walls of this box stand out in relief from a background which is engraved with a continuous swirl pattern. The enamelling technique used to achieve this encrusted effect resembles the cloisonne technique first used by the Ancient Egyptians to create mounts for the stones with which they decorated their jewellery. However, whereas the cloisons to hold the stones or enamel were usually produced by soldering a web of gold strip to the gold sheet, le Quin's cloisons are integral. Almost certainly they were produced by first raising areas of the gold above the background with a chaser's hammer and chisel, and then engraving away the smooth hollows to receive the flux. This is therefore in fact a *basse-taille* technique. Another *basse-taille* technique was used to produce an unusual effect on a box from the collection of Mr and Mrs Charles B. Wrightsman, which is now in the Victoria and Albert Museum. The box is decorated with bands of golden floral sprays, and the metal has been cut away round the sprays and filled with enamel to produce alternate olive-green and orange backgrounds to the flowers and leaves.

Of course, not all the enamelled boxes produced at this time were equally fine and now and again one comes across one on which the painting is badly composed or weakly drawn, but these are rare fallings-off from the general level of excellence. Tastelessness and over-elaboration are equally uncommon. Sometimes the

French makers did set diamonds and coloured gemstones in their boxes but usually only to enrich a thumbpiece as, for example, in that fine box which Jean George made in 1758, now in the Walters Art Gallery in Baltimore. This gold box is chased with marine scenes and has a diamond and emerald set thumbpiece, but even this degree of lavishness is uncommon, for by and large the French makers seem to have felt that even this restrained use of stones was an unnecessary gilding of the lily.

The subject matter of the enamel paintings was as varied as the techniques employed to bring colour to the French snuff box of the mid-eighteenth century. Flowers were perhaps the most popular of all subjects, but a close second were scenes of dalliances depicting lovers in some wooded grove. Then there were those scenes from village life much romanticised, showing men and women involved in pastoral pursuits as seen through urban eyes, which remind us that at this period French ladies of the court used to dress up as milkmaids to go on picnics. Martial and marine subjects were popular too, and so were scenes from the chase, and so too were the rather naïve Europeanised chinoiserie of the time. There is, for instance, a box in the Musée Cognacq-Jay in Paris of 1754 on the lid of which is depicted what can only be described as a Chinese *fête champêtre*, while Noël Hardivilliers had in the previous year produced an oval box decorated with bright blue *basse-taille* enamelling, showing Chinese musicians performing against the unlikely background of palm trees.

When one thinks of the French snuff boxes of this period, one's mind invariably conjures up these gold boxes enriched with enamel, but this was by no means the whole story. Integrally decorated gold boxes were still made in considerable numbers. Jean George, perhaps the most versatile of all the makers, produced not only some of the richest boxes, but some of the most restrained. His boxes, decorated with only a chased wavy linear pattern, enjoyed considerable fame and were known as *georgettes*.

Another popular method of decorating gold boxes at this time was to apply chased gold ornaments, usually in gold of a different colour from the body of the box. These ornaments had themes similar to those favoured by the enamel painters, and Kenneth Snowman, in his *Eighteenth Century Gold Boxes of Europe*,[1] illustrates

[1] Snowman, *op. cit.*

a particularly charming example of a box decorated in this way. It was made by Jean Frémin in 1760 and shows scenes of village life. This box is also interesting in illustrating a decorative technique which was to become an increasingly familiar feature of snuff boxes over the next hundred years. The French call this technique *guilloche*, but in English it has the more mundane name of engine-turning. It is in fact nothing more than mechanised engraving. The box was fixed in a clamp and moved by the machine against the sharp graver, a series of cams allowing many types of complicated linear designs to be produced.

Besides the gold and gold and enamel boxes, *en cage* boxes were made in considerable numbers at this time in Paris. The golden frames enclosed not only the stones and organic materials popular earlier in the century, but also imported and native lacquer work, ceramics, decorative glass and miniature paintings. It would appear from the records that many of these *en cage* boxes were made and sold by the merchants, the *marchands petits merciers* and *marchands de bimbeloterie*, who imported the panels or acquired them from local manufacturers and mounted them in gold frames bought in from the goldsmiths. The leading makers, however, clearly catered for this fashion themselves, for there are numbers of boxes bearing the marks of famous boxmakers who would have been unlikely to have employed middle men to make up and sell their wares.

Some of the most beautiful *en cage* boxes made in the 1750s were those set with lacquer panels imported by the East India Company. The finest examples came from Japan, but cheaper work was imported from Canton, and French lacquers imitating the oriental designs were produced in considerable quantities. The art of lacquering was developed in China, the tinted gum from the lacquer tree being applied to various grounds to produce a sleek surface not unlike an enamel. The Japanese lacquers which were used in the finest snuff boxes were black or sometimes red, with painted or raised gold decoration. Some of these lacquers had as many as thirty-six coats and might take half a year to produce.

One suspects that many of the lacquer panels used in the *en cage* boxes had been cut from already completed lacquer boxes and were not purpose-made. A box by Jean Frémin in the Walters Art Gallery in America certainly seems to confirm this, for the panels used for the sides give the impression of having been sawn down to fit. Another box in the Victoria and Albert Museum, by Pierre-François Drais also gives every indication of having been produced by dismembering an existing lacquer box.

When lacquer panels produced in France were used, gold motifs were sometimes pinned on to these, or piqué decorated panels inserted in them, as in the case of a box by Jean Ducrollay, Drais's apprentice, now in the Victoria and Albert Museum, which was marked in 1754 and 1755. The red lacquer panels which comprise this box have had black lacquer inserts let into them on which birds are depicted in piqué, while the gold frame has a rose and leaf motif in *basse-taille* enamel. This technique of inlaying lacquer in lacquer seems to have appealed to Ducrollay, for there is a similar box bearing his mark in the Metropolitan Museum of Art.

The most famous of the many attempts to produce a satisfactory substitute for oriental lacquer in France was the glazed varnish developed by the four brothers Martin, known as Vernis Martin. It is difficult to judge the effectiveness of Vernis Martin today, because it proved to have the disadvantage of discolouring with age, but there is no doubt the Martins' contemporaries thought highly of their invention. They were called in to decorate Madame de Pompadour's apartments at Versailles and covered the walls with delicate lacquers. These apartments were cluttered with testimony to Madame's understanding patronage of artists and craftsmen, a patronage which is said to have cost Louis XV 36 million livres. Some of this money went to pay for the hundreds of snuff boxes that she collected, among which perhaps were examples of the work of the Martins on a smaller scale, and one of which was certainly that box with the King's portrait on the lid, given to her after he had been taken ill in her bed and seemed likely to die there.

Jean George, who experimented successfully with so many techniques, made boxes in tortoise-shell which were decorated with piqué of great charm and delicacy and worked in *quatre-couleur* gold. He also produced the most feminine of enamel boxes and bought numbers of ceramic panels from the Sèvres porcelain factory to mount as boxes. How attractive the results were can be seen from a surviving example in the Louvre illustrated in plate 9. In the centre of the panels little *putti* recline on clouds and these pictures are enclosed by borders of that incredible Sèvres green. For these panels George produced perfectly proportioned mounts, chased with a pattern of flowers, ribbons and acanthus.

Probably it was the difficulty of obtaining large sheets of mother-of-pearl that suggested to the boxmaker the idea of using this material to produce intricate mosaics, the parts of which are held in place by a spider's web of gold. A relatively restrained example of this technique is the box by Charles le Bastier in the Victoria and Albert Museum, which is composed of leaf-shaped segments of mother-of-pearl. These segments are carved so that their surfaces flash the iridescent colours, an effect caused by the interference of light by the platy structure of the calcite. More typical of this use of mother-of-pearl is that *tour de force* in the Musée Cognacq-Jay, which has superimposed over a mosaic a reclining woman surrounded by plump *amorini* in chased gold. Behind these figures there is a shell shape inlaid with red agate. Another fascinating example of this technique is in the Louvre, a box of Jean Gaillard who used mother-of-pearl, tinted shell and cornelian to construct mosaics representing architectural façades.

Mother-of-pearl was also used, usually together with other shell and ivory, to produce appliqué allegorical designs, chinoiseries and *scènes galantes* of great complexity which were applied to gold panels. These are not the happiest products of the age, for the technique often condemns the rendering of the figures to be somewhat stiff, and some of these boxes are also rather garish. A better use of this method of decoration, probably because it is apt to the subject, is to be seen on a deep oblong box made in Paris about 1760 and now in a private collection in New York. The gold panels which form the lid and walls of this box have been engine-turned with a wavy pattern which suggests the sea, and applied to these panels are nautical trophies in tinted mother-of-pearl. Scattered over the rest of the panels are reproductions of a variety of shells also carved in tinted mother-of-pearl, executed in such detail that they remind one of the drawings from some guide to the crustaceans. But the most spectacular example of this style of decoration is on a box in the collection of Baron Elsie de Rothschild, from the workshop of Noël Hardivilliers. The panels of this box are of rich lapis lazuli, encrusted with chinoiseries in tinted mother-of-pearl. Most effective perhaps is the base on which are depicted two quarrelling dragons in a typical Chinese rockscape.

During the 1760s and 1770s there was a vogue for deep oblong *en cage* boxes, often with canted corners, the panels of which consisted of views painted in gouache and placed behind glass panels. The gouache painters chose a variety of subjects: river scenes and scenes from village life and town life and hunting scenes; but most popular of all were the views of the great châteaux of France. The most favoured of these gouache artists whose work is featured on snuff boxes, was Louis-Nicolas van Blarenberghe, who started his career as a marine painter. His paintings are incredibly detailed almost to the point of fussiness, and neither his colouring nor his rendering of figures is beyond criticism, but his work was greatly in demand at the time. His most famous, though perhaps not his best works, were his panels for two boxes made for the Duc de Choiseul, the protégé of Madame de Pompadour, who became Prime Minister of France and was an avid collector of Dutch paintings. One of these boxes features views of Choiseul's famous château at Chanteloup near Amboise and its impressively laid out grounds that rivalled those at Versailles. The other is the box on every surface of which is depicted a different interior view of the Duc's Paris house. In his gouaches for this box, Van Blarenberghe features his patron's collection of paintings, and many of these pictures, the largest of which occupies only 1·5 by 2 millimetres, are actually identifiable.

Meanwhile during the 1760s there had been a dramatic change in the style of the enamelled gold snuff boxes. The discoveries at Pompeii and Herculaneum ushered in a new classical revival. New forms and new motifs were distilled from the shattered remnants of these once prosperous Roman towns. During the two previous decades a few round and oval boxes had been made, but relatively few. From 1760 up to the Revolution it was the oblong snuff box which was to be the exception. The typical box of the second half of the eighteenth century was an oval box. In the centre of the lid a plaque was placed in a decorative surround. This central motif was bracketed by two areas of translucent enamel, usually laid over engine-turning. Round the edge of the lid was a complex mount or decorative border, usually enriched with *basse-taille* enamel work. The high sides of this typical box played a very important rôle in the design. They were the walls of a little temple made for the worship of snuff, and so what more logical than that pilasters should be placed round them, sometimes literally interpreted but more often freely rendered. Alternatively, Vitruvian arches or classical statues on plinths or rows of husks were placed round these walls. Between these neo-classical architectural clichés there were panels of enamel, and set into these panels smaller versions of the plaque on the lid were sometimes placed.

These boxes were sometimes described as Louis Seize, but they in fact became fashionable more than a decade before Louis XV died and was succeeded by the unfortunate Louis XVI. Some of the old masters, not surprisingly the adaptable Jean George among them, took up the new style. One of the most interesting and charming of his boxes from this period featured the new type of decoration which had its roots in rediscovered Rome. On this box, which was made between 1759 and 1762, there appear on the lid and on the sides *grisaille* paintings by the principal exponent of painting *en camaïeu* in tones of grey, Mlle Duplessis. George gave the rather naïve plaque on the lid a frame of diamonds and provided the box with a superb clasp in the form of a bow encrusted with the same stones. George, unlike most of his French contemporaries, seems to have come to like diamonds, and one oval box he produced, now in the Rijksmuseum in Amsterdam, looks as though it had been dipped in them. Nothing could be further removed from those simple little *georgettes* for which he had once been famous.

A new generation of master craftsmen, tested by the goldsmiths' Guild and found skilful, appeared on the scene at this time and the marks of Jean-Joseph Barrière, Louis-Philippe Demay, Charles le Bastier and Pierre-François Drais appeared on the new boxes. These also bore the charge and décharge marks of the Fermiers généraux of the time: the portcullis and shell of Eloy Brichard, the crossed laurels and dog's head of Jean-Jacques Prévost, and the floral cluster and helmeted head of Julien Alaterre. These four makers produced many variations on the theme of the oval box. When in 1766, for instance, Demay produced that superb box, now in the Louvre, he eschewed the architectural motifs. Instead, he commissioned Charles-Jacques de Mailly to decorate it with allegorical *grisailles* surrounded by exquisitely delineated flowers.

The enamellers at this time began to vie with nature, producing more or less plausible imitations of lapis lazuli, or of dendritic agate with its moss and tree-like inclusions, or of the marbles in all their variety. On a box in the Metropolitan Museum bearing the mark of Barrière, the enameller has even had the temerity to try to simulate the subtle greens and the complex striations of malachite. It was hardly surprising that he was not particularly successful. More effective by far than these attempts to simulate stones were the silk and moiré effects that the enamellers devised by laying layers of translucent enamel over suitably engine-turned grounds. From this period too came the leopard-skin boxes, which were enamelled a curious yellow-pink dappled with what can only be described as blue blotches. Though not very convincing, these boxes must have been popular, it seems, for there are examples in both the Louvre and in the Rijksmuseum.

The medallions on the lids of these oval boxes depicted a variety of subjects in a variety of techniques. Besides the allegorical paintings *en grisailles*, the enameller also depicted gods, goddesses and attendant *amorini* in rich colours. Many of these boxes were portrait boxes with miniatures held in oval frames behind a protective glass on the lids. A box bearing a miniature portrait of Louis XIV under glass in the Louvre collection is also interesting as it illustrates two decorative techniques which became popular in the 1770s. Areas of this box, which bears the mark of Paul-Nicolas Menière, are covered with rich blue enamel scattered with gold stars. These stars had been evolved by a Geneva enameller, Jean Coteau. Coteau's *paillons*, as these stars are sometimes called, were cut out from thin gold foil and fused into the enamel. The border of this box is also decorated with little enamel flowers in relief, interspersed with little blobs of white enamel simulating half-pearls. This flower and pearl motif was a characteristic feature of many boxes made in Paris during the 1770s. Another popular feature was the addition of swags and garlands of chased gold to link the various decorative elements of the decoration, and

1. Silver boxes from last quarter of seventeenth century; English. James Walker Collection.

2. Two late seventeenth-century Italian silver snuff boxes. Victoria and Albert Museum.

3. Pressed horn Drake box by John Obrisset, early eighteenth century. London Museum.

4. Snuff flasks and horns made from late eighteenth century up to the mid-nineteenth. The dating of individual examples is almost impossible. National Museum, Finland.

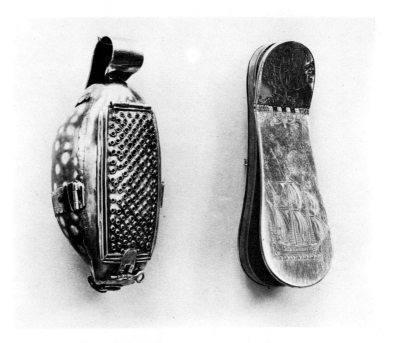

5. Silver snuff rasp, early eighteenth century, and snuff rasp made from a cowrie shell. Victoria and Albert Museum.

6. Baroque form box by Daniel Gouers made in three colours of gold with chased ornament against a matted ground, and set with diamonds and emeralds. Inside the lid is a portrait of Louis XV in armour. 1727. Louvre, Paris.

7. Gold *en cage* box with inlays in Japanese lacquer made by Adrien Vachette in 1785. Louvre, Paris.

8. *En cage* box with black lacquer panels decorated with *pique d'or* work made between 1761/63 by Jean-Marie Tiron. Louvre, Paris.

9. Jean George mounted panels from the Royal pottery of Sevres in this gold *en cage* box. 1759/60. Louvre, Paris.

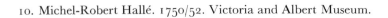

10. Michel-Robert Hallé. 1750/52. Victoria and Albert Museum.

11. (three views) Gold snuff box chased by George Michael Moser about 1760. It illustrates Reynold's description of him as "the first gold chaser in the kingdom". Christie's.

12. Engraved and chased gold box decorated with blue *basse-taille* enamel. English 1776/7. Victoria and Albert Museum.

13. Silver box made by Edward Cornock in 1723/4. Victoria and Albert Museum.

among the boxes owned by Madame de Pompadour were listed "*boîtes-à-guirlandes*".

Sometimes the medallions used on the oval snuff boxes might be no more than trophies, allegories, or contemporary *scènes repoussées* chased on the lid itself. Or they might take the form of applied gold motifs, usually in a colour of gold different from that used to fabricate the box itself. Sometimes these applied motifs were little circular hinged lids hiding a surprise. If one pressed a button the lid would flick open and a bright bird would appear to pirouette, flapping its wings stiffly and carolling a song. Singing bird boxes were probably not a Swiss invention, as they are often thought to be, but a French one. Sometimes when the little lid opened it was not a bird that stood revealed but a watch dial, surrounded perhaps with a sumptuous nimbus of diamonds. Earlier, in 1745, Louis XV had ordered a watch to be set in the lid of a snuff box which he intended to present to Madame Poisson, the mother of his mistress, Madame de Pompadour. Unfortunately in 1745 Madame Poisson died, and to the wry amusement of the court, Louis then gave the box instead to his wife, that most pathetic of queens, Marie Leczinska. One might have expected that this novel combination of watch and snuff box, which many people find particularly charming, would subsequently have become very much *à la mode*. A number of makers did indeed produce such boxes now and again over the next fifty years, but they never became very popular because the watches, existing in the dusty surroundings of a snuff box, would soon have ceased to tell the time. Dust is a watch's worst enemy!

Not all the snuff boxes made after 1760 were oval. For instance, oblong boxes with gouache paintings and other types of panels mounted *en cage* remained popular for another decade. Many of these later *en cage* boxes, for which there was a considerable vogue in the 1780s, had canted corners with architectural motifs at the angles. Adrien-Jean-Maximilien Vachette, a well-known maker of these boxes, produced a number which look at first glance to be set *en cage* with malachite or agate, but which on closer inspection prove to be enamelled.

Perhaps it is hindsight that makes us perceive a certain decadence in the boxes made during the waning years of the century, as if those who fashioned them had lost their enthusiasm and become dispirited, repeating over and over again, each time with a little less conviction, the by now time-worn clichés. The craftsmanship remained impeccable—the Guild saw to that. It was the artistic inspiration which began to flag as the clouds of revolution gathered over Paris.

When the revolution eventually came there was, of course, no longer any demand for such aristocratic symbols as gold snuff boxes. The revolution also swept away the old medieval guild system, which whatever its faults must be given some of the credit for the incredibly high standard of the gold boxes which had been made during the foregoing century. The craft was placed under Government control and anyone who aspired to do so might become a goldsmith. Though some fine gold boxes were to be produced in Paris when things returned to normal, these cannot bear comparison with the boxes that had been produced during the eighteenth century under the stringent régime of the guild.

What is surprising is that so many eighteenth-century French boxes survived the revolution. Goldsmiths' wares, as has been mentioned before, are particularly susceptible in troubled times, and in a period when palaces and châteaux were plundered in the name of democracy and even the tombs of France's ancient kings were desecrated, a lot of beautiful boxes must have gone into the melting pot. But many fine examples of the goldsmith's art did survive the débâcle somehow, a minor miracle for which those of us who are fascinated by snuff boxes are duly thankful.

The gold boxes tend to overshadow all else, but they were obviously not the only receptacles for snuff made during the eighteenth century in France. There were many snuff-takers among those of modest means, people who could afford at best a silver box or possibly a porcelain one from Saint-Cloud or one of the other potteries that produced snuff boxes. Kenneth Snowman lists some of the other alternatives to gold.[1] There were *boîtes-à-la-bergamotes* made of wood and lined with orange peel. There were boxes covered in shagreen, including those *momenti-mori* boxes made following the death of Louis XV and known as *la consolation dans le chagrin*. There were wooden and horn boxes, many of which had royal portraits and contemporary motifs impressed into them, but including also the *tabatière-à-la-silhouette* made after 1759,

[1] *Ibid.*

66

named for the "shadowy" Contrôleur Général de Finances, Etienne de Silhouette, who was dismissed from his office after a year because he bored the King. There were the *Bouronnes*, carved from the roots of elm and box, popularised by a Monsieur Bouron of Grenoble. There were *tabatières en Pomponne* made of copper, and even cardboard boxes called *platitudes* because of their flat form, or sometimes known as *turgotines* after that Monsieur Turgot, who was to be responsible for temporarily suppressing the Paris Guild of Goldsmiths in 1776, and who became infamous for introducing stringent fiscal measures in the reign of Louis XVI.

Besides being used as panels for *en cage* boxes, Vernis Martin and the similar concoctions produced by other *peintres vernissers* were used to produce *tabatière de Martin*. These were papier-mâché boxes, called *carton vernis* in France, and usually round or oval in form. The paper was pressed over a wooden core, and then painted with a lacquer based on copal resin. The rims of these boxes were protected by silver gilt mounts, or occasionally gold ones were used. Many of them had tortoise-shell liners, and the paintings that decorated these boxes were similar in content to the enamel paintings on the gold boxes, portraits and figure groups predominating, but allegories were painted on them as well, like that in a box in the Louvre which features Europa and a rather placid-looking bull with a garland round its neck. Indeed France produced snuff boxes made from every conceivable material with one notable exception. Copper boxes decorated with painted enamels, which were produced in large numbers in England, Germany and Scandinavia, were rather surprisingly not produced in France.

As might be expected, the makers of the silver snuff boxes copied the form and decoration of the fashionable French gold boxes. The earlier baroque box gave place to the rococo box, and then in the 1740s the oblong box became fashionable in silver as well as in gold, and in the 1760s this was superseded by the oval box. But on the silver boxes the decoration was always integral rather than applied, the various motifs, the *fête champêtre*, fruits and flowers, the battle scenes, the scenes of the chase, the allegorical figure groups were in the form of chased repoussé, or flat-chased into the surface, or later cut into it with a sharp graver. A baroque-form silver box submitted by Antoine Daroux to the

Mint in 1745 and completed in 1746 has diagonal bands of chased leaf and flower decoration on it, reminiscent of fashionable enamelled boxes of the period, though much has been lost by the absence of colour. Daroux provided the less wealthy customers too with silver *en cage* boxes, like that one in the A La Vieille Russie collection in New York, but again the purchasers of the silver box were getting something second-rate, for the chinoiserie lacquer panels inlaid with mother-of-pearl are rather mediocre. Poor in quality too are mother-of-pearl panels, inlaid with tinted shell and used for a silver *en cage* box in the Brooklyn Museum.

Sometimes fine silver boxes were enriched with applied gold motifs, as was an oval box of 1760–61 by Louis Charonnat, now in the Metropolitan Museum collection. Sometimes too the silver was inlaid with gold as in a fine oblong box of the same date by that famous maker Charles le Bastier. Another silver box of high quality is illustrated by Bo Bramsen in his *Nordiske Snusdaser*.[1] This box from a Danish private collection is a replica of the fashionable oval gold box of the 1770s in the neo-classical style. There is the inevitable central medallion on the lid, this one in the form of a chased floral trophy. Round this is a chased garland and beyond are engine-turned areas, but these are left bare and not covered with enamel as they would have been on a gold box. All this is contained within a formal border, and the sides of the box are decorated with areas of engine-turning between the usual chased pilasters.

The potteries at Saint-Cloud were the first to produce porcelain snuff boxes in France. Saint-Cloud boxes were being advertised as early as 1731, and the factory continued to produce them for the next twenty years. Other potteries producing snuff boxes during the eighteenth century were Crépy-le-Valois, Mennecy and Chantilly, the latter of which is credited with the introduction of those boxes in the forms of shoes and figurines, apparently much in demand for a time, but whether they were intended for snuff is debatable. Sèvres snuff boxes are extremely rare, but as has been seen this pottery did contribute panels to some of the most elegant snuff boxes of the age produced by Jean George.

The Musée des Arts Décoratifs in the Louvre has a number of the productions of Saint-Cloud in its collection. This pottery

[1] Bramsen, *op. cit.*

produced in the 1730s included many boxes painted with chinoiseries, rather stilted chinoiseries reminiscent of those chased and engraved on English Caroline silverware. One of the boxes in the collection of the museum in this style has a body in the form of a shallow cup with a flat lid. Lid and body were fitted with metal mounts that developed into the hinge at the back. Saint-Cloud also produced porcelain boxes of baroque form. Mennecy produced boxes in the 1750s in the fashionable oblong shape, and then in the following decade made oval ones. Vincennes, which produced boxes during the 1750s, specialised in rather tall fancy shapes, and some of these boxes were fitted with gold mounts made by Paris goldsmiths.

CHAPTER THREE

EIGHTEENTH-CENTURY ENGLISH GOLD
AND SILVER BOXES

No great number of English gold and silver boxes from the first two decades of the new century have survived, and most of those that have resemble those silver boxes made at the tail end of the seventeenth century. The later boxes differ only in being more urbane than their predecessors, as befitted the products of a new, self-consciously elegant age. The hinges and thumbpieces are less obtrusive. The decoration, still usually no more than a coat of arms or a monogram, was more formalised and usually better executed.

A typical, if unusually fine gold box, that bears out the similarity between the boxes made in the old century and the new one, was that sold at Christie's some years ago, with the Lockwood arms elegantly chased on the slightly domed oval lid. This was made about 1720. Another gold box of similar form made about a decade earlier is in the collection of the Antique Porcelain Company in New York, and this has a very florid monogram as the only decoration on the lid. Yet another shallow oval gold box in the seventeenth-century style from this period is the one with a portrait of Mary Queen of Scots on the lid, with the combined arms of Cotton and Craggs on the base, which is in the Victoria and Albert Museum collection in London. In this brief inventory of the rare gold boxes from the early years of the century mention must be made of a similar oval box (made about 1705) in the collection of Kenneth Snowman, embellished with a fine example of John Obrisset's work, a tortoise-shell plaque with a fine pressed bust of Charles I let into the lid. Then there is a box from a private collection, illustrated by Kenneth Snowman in his *Eighteenth Century Gold Boxes of Europe*,[1] a shallow oblong box with rounded corners again decked out with a fine coat of arms, in

[1] Snowman, *op. cit.*

this case those of the Earl of Lytton. Finally there is a box, possibly slightly later in date in the Walters Art Gallery in Baltimore. This is a shell-shaped double box, and the lid decoration immediately strikes one as not being English. It is in fact English, but was copied from a design by the Nuremberg artist, Paul Decker the Younger. The box was made in London for the Duke of Chandos early in the 1720s.

From 1730 onwards those high relief repoussé gold boxes of baroque shape which one thinks of as characteristically English began to appear. They are very similar to those produced in Holland in the middle years of the eighteenth century, and the Dutch boxes are known to be the work of Huguenot craftsmen who sought refuge from religious persecution in Amsterdam. One cannot help but wonder if the chasers who decorated the English boxes may not also have been, like so many of the finest of the eighteenth-century English silversmiths, Huguenots. Possibly also some of them could have been Germans or Italians. England in the eighteenth century offered not only a good deal more religious freedom than did most of the continental countries, but also the promise of solid patronage from a wealthy aristocracy and a newly influential merchant class. So foreign artists and craftsmen flocked to England to paint the ceilings of palladian mansions, to encrust them with ornate plaster work and to provide prospects littered with statuary to be viewed from windows and terraces. It would not be surprising therefore if the lords and ladies and the merchants and bankers and their wives should have employed the services of men who had learnt their skill in raising allegories and biblical scenes on gold sheet in continental workshops. There is some evidence too to support this supposition. The only chasers whose names are recorded are Gastrell, Manby, Bingant and Moser. The only one of this quartet about whom we know more than his name is George Michael Moser. Joshua Reynolds described him as "the first gold chaser in the kingdom" and he came originally from the old walled town of Schaffhausen on the banks of the Rhine in Switzerland. He was a man of many talents, a founder member of the Royal Academy and a noted painter as well as a chaser. As for the other three, Bingant's name suggests he was certainly of French origin, and Gastrell and Manby sound like anglicisations of French names.

So we are driven to suspect that though the eighteenth-century repoussé gold snuff boxes may be of English make, that characteristic decoration was more than likely the work of foreign chasers, chasers who also decorated the typically English repoussé gold watch cases of the time. When one really looks at the chasing on many of these boxes, one has to admit that it is not particularly English in character. Those perspectives of classical ruins, those lovers among rococo scrolls, the allegories, the neo-Roman figure groups are all reminiscent of French designs, and of course the baroque and rococo shapes in which the boxes were made derived from France too. The decoration and the form of these boxes could have been borrowed, of course, from pattern books by English craftsmen intent on pleasing a taste for continental art acquired by patrons who had done the Grand Tour. Some of them could be copies of the work of emigré craftsmen. Indeed, the facts about how these boxes came to be produced will probably never be known. They will almost certainly remain one of the unsolved mysteries of the history of craftsmanship.

Some of these eighteenth-century English boxes really are superb, as fine as anything made in Paris, and outstanding among them was the work of Moser. Identifiable examples of Moser's work are rare, but those that do exist are incomparable examples of the chaser's art, proving that Reynolds's estimate of his ability was no mere empty compliment to a fellow Academician. There is for example a box which bears the signature "G.M. Moser feint" on the lid in a private collection in New York. This box, incidentally, also bears the initials "P.R.", which are believed to be those of Philip Roker, the goldsmith who actually made the box that Moser decorated, a further proof, if proof were needed, that maker and chaser were seldom if ever one and the same person.

The delineation of the figures on many repoussé boxes lacks any great artistic merit. They are usually rather spiritless. Nobody could say this of Moser's lively rendering of Porsena, King of Klusi, watching Mucius putting his hand into the flaming brazier on the lid of Philip Roker's box. The figure of Father Tiber protecting the she-wolf and Romulus and Remus on the base is equally vigorous. The composition of these little vignettes is masterly too, but even more impressive perhaps is the way in which

Moser breathes life into the formal imagery of the decoration that surrounds them. And how different from the usual run of decorative detail is that trophy surmounted by an eagle with outstretched wings on the wall of the box below the thumbpiece. Even the little laurel garland that flows out of this trophy is beautifully conceived and immaculately chased. This 11·5 cm. × 9 cm. box is undoubtedly a work of art in gold, but it also claims our attention as a feat of craftsmanship. The chasing would have taken weeks and it is hard to credit, looking at the box, that the work was done with nothing but a hammer and some punches and chisels. The lid that Roker had made, the metal flat and unadorned, would have been laid face down on a bed of molten pitch which when dry would support it while yet having some give in it. The chaser would then have embossed the box with punches, driving up the raised areas against the resistance of the pitch. Then he would have turned over the lid and bedded it down on pitch again. Then he would have begun to create the detail painstakingly with hammer and little chisels selected from the hundreds of different ones on his bench. Each blow of the hammer would have been precisely struck to push away just the right amount of gold with the point of the chisel, otherwise the lines would have looked ragged. And this exacting work would have gone on hour after hour, day in and day out.

Another example of Moser's skill as a chaser can be seen on B/W plate 11, a bombé-form box which he embellished with a riot of baroque cliché, superbly delineated.

Other English makers, though none of them surpassed Moser, produced gold repoussé boxes of great charm and superb craftsmanship. One thinks of that little purse-shaped box with rococo decoration in the Museum of Fine Arts in Boston, produced about 1750 by a maker known only by his initials P.P. And there is a superbly chased shaped oblong box in the A La Vieille Russie collection in New York from the same period, with allegorical figures and a temple on a rock in a sunburst surround in the background, all enclosed in delicate scrolls. One recalls also a fine deep oblong box with canted corners in the collection of Charles Clore, again made about 1750. This is formed of red and green gold and the figures and architectural motifs stand out from flat-chased whorls that suggest gathering banks of cumulus clouds.

73

The English makers also produced some fine boxes in the *en cage* style. There is a very pretty rococo *en cage* box in the Hermitage in Leningrad, with lacquerwork simulating malachite under glass held in an ornate trellis-work frame, which is believed to be English. And there is another trellis-work box of about 1763, which was presented to Thomas Dimsdale by the Empress Catherine of Russia after he had inoculated her and her son against the smallpox. The maker of this box used panels of rich red agate, and his trellis-work frame is a riot of floral and foliate motifs, architectural details, finely chased and with contrasting areas of bright and matt finishing. A box made about 1760 in the form of a sphinx carved from agate and enriched with diamond-set gold mounts in the Clore collection, bears witness to the fact that the English boxmakers were capable of fantasy and extravagance, too. It has been suggested that these figure boxes, a number of which exist, were made from imported carvings done by foreign glyptic artists, probably Germans, for hardstone carving of this kind was a continental rather than an English craft.

In the 1760s the English makers were forced at last to give up their baroque shapes and repoussé chasing in favour of the oval form and the enamel decoration of the Louis Seize style, which from its birthplace in France had swept through Europe. Even Moser could no longer find customers for his chasing. As Joan Evans put it in her *History of Jewellery*,[1] he "had to transfer his skill to the production of figure compositions in enamel because of the change of fashion". He also employed the artist Augustin Toussaint to produce classical vignettes for him, and signed examples of the work of this fine artist have survived.

Some of the repoussé boxes had had miniature portraits inside their lids, while the rakes and fops predictably had "had lustful postures obscenely drawn in every box". From 1760 onwards the miniature painter's contribution was moved from the obscurity of the interior and was given pride of place upon the lid, where it often formed the central medallion of the neo-classical decoration. Work by artists of the standing of Richard Cosway and George Morland is to be found on snuff boxes from this period.

George Michael Moser had a nephew, Joseph Moser, who worked with him, and at one time some of the finest boxes of the

[1] Evans, Joan, *A History of Jewellery*, London, 1953.

74

neo-classical period were believed to have been his work. It turns out, however, that the initials J.M. on these were not in fact his. They were those of James Morriset, a maker of small wares of Huguenot descent, who first registered his mark in 1787. He is best known perhaps as the maker of the beautiful little oval freedom box in the National Maritime Museum at Greenwich with an enamel painting of the Battle of the Nile on the lid. Kenneth Snowman illustrates an equally impressive example of his work, however.[1] This is an oval snuff box made in the 1780s which has a gold plaque depicting a scene from Shakespeare's *The Tempest* in a blue enamel frame on the lid. There were other fine boxes made in England at this time: a nice portrait box in the Royal Scottish Museum in Edinburgh comes to mind, and that very English-looking box in the Victoria and Albert Museum, covered with delicate flower sprays in blue *basse-taille* enamel (plate 12). In general though the English work in the Louis Seize style looks a bit provincial, almost invariably lacking the conviction of the French originals.

Like the early gold boxes, the early eighteenth-century silver boxes were similar to those from the previous age, oval with flat or slightly domed lids. One can compare, for example, two boxes in the Victoria and Albert Museum which illustrate the similarities of style between a box made about 1680 and one made about 1720. Both are oval and both are decorated with rather sketchy engraving, which has been described as "scratch engraving", and is possibly the result of Dutch influence. The decoration on the earlier box is more naïve, consisting of an ill-drawn monogram round which are depicted a carrier's wagon drawn by six horses, a man on horseback, a traveller on foot and a distant prospect of the city of Norwich. The eighteenth-century box, the work of Edward Cornock, has a better executed representation of two fishermen on a foreshore. This later box also has a bold flange round the lid which gives the box a greater feeling of substance. This flange had become a feature of boxes by the 1720s, and can be seen on a second box in the Victoria and Albert Museum, another product of Cornock's workshop, decorated with a fine coat of arms. It is interesting how this small addition gives the box an eighteenth-century air. It looks quite different from, say,

[1] Snowman, *op cit.*

that extraordinary William III snuff box with its odd Jacobite imagery made by Lawrence Coles in 1697, and illustrated in Eric Delieb's *Silver Boxes*.[1] One is unmistakably a product of the seventeenth century. The other obviously belongs to the age of the Earl of Burlington, of Thomas Kent and Pierre Harache.

With some exceptions the English silver snuff boxes of the eighteenth century are disappointing. When one considers how many fine silverwares were produced in England during those hundred years, many of the boxes seem rather uninspired by comparison. What is more, surprisingly few silver boxes seem to have been made. One would have expected there to be an abundance of them. Probably their rarity is explained by the fact that the English snuffers had so many alternatives to choose from. There were the pinchbeck boxes which were plausible imitations of gold ones. There were the cheaper but equally attractive and serviceable boxes made from Sheffield plate, and of course there were those painted enamel copper boxes produced in such numbers in the course of the century, not to mention iron boxes, brass boxes and papier-mâché boxes.

It was not until late in the century that the silver snuff box really enjoyed any great popularity in England, when attractive boxes began to be produced in great quantities by specialist makers in Birmingham and in London. Though good examples of eighteenth-century silver boxes are rare, they are well worth searching for because although the silver boxes which have come down to us may be less accomplished, they are more individualistic and much less influenced by continental fashions than the gold boxes of the period. Most of the silver boxes were lightly decorated, usually with engraving or flat chasing. Only the odd box has repoussé-chased decoration. It has been suggested that silver does not lend itself to this type of decoration, but this theory is surely refuted by the hundreds of Scandinavian silver boxes which were decorated in this way, and by the rococo extravaganzas that Paul de Lamerie produced for the tables of the nobility.

The majority of English silver boxes are also simple in form, either oval or oblong, the oblong ones frequently having canted corners. A feature of many English boxes was that they were hinged on the top rather than on the end. An oval box made by

[1] Delieb, *op. cit.*

76

James Smith about 1725 has an oval lid which covers not more than a quarter of the area of the top of the box, but more usually the lid extends over about three-quarters of the box. The Smith box is interesting also in that besides foliate engraving on the top and the lid it has bead decoration round the edge and round the rim of the lid. Bead decoration appears on a number of silver boxes made during the first thirty years of the century, including an oblong box of 1716 that was in the Parke-Bernet sale in 1970.

Sometimes the silver boxmakers became more ambitious, prompted perhaps by a discerning patron, and produced boxes of more complex form. Baroque and shell-shaped boxes do turn up occasionally. For example, there is a beautiful example of a shell-shaped silver box made in 1730, in the Victoria and Albert Museum, decorated with formal foliate engraving and bearing a monogram. In the middle years of the century a few deep snuff boxes appeared with incurved sides. There is a small silver-mounted ivory one, with an octagonal lid, in the James Walker collection, *c.* 1720, and another one with a cabochon agate in the lid *c.* 1760 (see plate 14). A very similar box to this last is in the collection of Karel Citroen in Amsterdam, but the chasing on this one suggests that it is of German or Scandinavian rather than of English make. Bo Bramsen also illustrates a number of these deep incurved boxes made in Scandinavia in the middle of the century, and as the box in the James Walker collection is not marked there is a possibility that this is not English but Scandinavian work. The assignment of unmarked silver boxes is sometimes as difficult as the assignment of those made from organic materials.

A number of English silver snuff boxes made in the 1760s had stones mounted in the lids, usually striated agates. Sometimes the lids consisted of a stone mounted in a narrow bezel, but more often the stone formed a central motif, the wide silver surround being flat-chased with formal decoration. These agates came mostly from Scotland and were polished by lapidaries in Aberdeen. The massive fluorspar, found at Castleford in Derbyshire and called Blue John, was used for panels in English *en cage* boxes. Marble panels were used too, and marble mosaics, made from pieces of this many-coloured material cemented together. Boxes with panels of highly finished slate, japanned and painted, have been found, and even coal was used to make snuff boxes. The coal used was the bituminous "cannel coal" or "parrot coal", that takes a high polish. As early as 1697 Celia Fiennes on a visit to Newcastle-under-Lyme saw "shining Channel coale . . . that is hard and will be pollish'd like black marble for salts or snuff boxes or such like". Boxes were still being made 154 years later from this material, for some were exhibited at the Great Exhibition in 1851.

Throughout the century, too, silver boxes were fitted with lids of mother-of-pearl or of ivory or tortoise-shell decorated with piqué work. Silver-mounted cowrie shells were popular in England from about 1760 onwards. They were provided with a flat lid hinged on top and decorated with flat chasing, engraving or bright cutting, often featuring a coat-of-arms (plate 17).

Towards the end of the century English smallworkers in silver produced some oval boxes in the Louis Seize style, some of them peculiar in having the English style top hinge (plate 18). Perfectly plain examples are found, but sometimes they were chased all over. A lightly chased example is in the James Walker collection dated 1789 and inscribed Samuel Nicholas, Leominster (plate 19). This box is most unusual in having a hinged magnifying glass which tucks into a recess in the base. Another eighteenth-century oddity is a plain silver box in the form of a keystone, made about 1770, and illustrated by Delieb, who suggests it was probably a Masonic box.

THE MARKS ON BRITISH BOXES

Though few early eighteenth-century British gold and silver boxes were hallmarked, from the later part of the eighteenth century onwards virtually all of them were. A knowledge of British hallmarks can therefore be very useful to collectors.

There are five marks which a collector should be on the look-out for on boxes ascribed to English makers. These are the quality mark, the town mark, the date letter, the maker's mark and the duty mark (as shown below).

THE QUALITY MARK

The same quality mark was used for both gold, of the required standard of 22 carat, and sterling silver up to 1797–8. This mark took the form of a lion *passant guardant*, a standing lion with its head turned to face outwards.

After 1797–8, when the minimum permitted standard for goldwares was reduced to 18 carat, new standard marks for gold were introduced. From this period all the English offices, except Sheffield which assayed virtually no gold in the snuff-box period, stamped 18 carat goldwares with a crown and the figure 18. If a boxmaker continued to use the old 22 carat standard the offices marked his wares with a crown and the figure 22 after 1844. From 1854 onwards there were lower standards—9, 12 and 15 carat—and these were marked with the appropriate carat number. Next to this another figure expressed the gold content of the alloy in parts per thousand. Boxes made of 9 carat gold were marked with the figure 9 in a lozenge, followed by the figures 375 in another lozenge, for example.

For sterling silverwares, the lion *passant guardant* continued in use, except that after 1875 the lion on London and Birmingham wares no longer looked sideways and became a lion *passant*. On silverwares made between 1697 and 1720, and occasionally even after that, one may find a quite different quality mark, that of the higher Britannia standard. In the late seventeenth century it had become a common malpractice to clip the sterling silver shillings and to sell the clippings to silversmiths. To discourage this William III raised the minimum permitted standard of silver from 925 parts per 1000 to 958·4 parts per thousand pure in 1697. This would have involved any silversmith buying clippings from the coinage and further refining these and this is a very exacting and complicated process. This higher standard of silver bore the standard mark of a lion's head with a ragged neck, known in heraldry as a lion's head erased. London also changed her town mark for silverware between 1697 and 1720, using a seated figure of Britannia. It has been known, incidentally, for people to confuse this mark with the rather similar Hibernia mark used by the Dublin assay office.

THE TOWN MARK

Though a number of the smaller towns marked plate during the eighteenth century, as far as gold and silver snuff boxes are concerned the only town marks likely to be met with are those of London, Birmingham, Sheffield and Chester. The Birmingham mark is shown on page 78.

The town mark used by London, except on Britannia silver, was a leopard's head in a shield. Up to 1821 the leopard's head bore a crown, but after that it was uncrowned. Chester used the city arms, a shield bearing three wheat sheaves, as a town mark and up to 1839 a leopard's head as well; crowned up to 1822 and uncrowned thereafter. Birmingham, which received a royal charter in 1773, permitting plate to be assayed and marked in the city, adopted an anchor town mark. Sheffield which received its royal charter in the same year used a crown mark as its town mark.

THE DATE LETTER

All the assay offices stamped a date letter into wares sent to them for assay, to indicate the year of marking. When the office had run through one alphabet they adopted another one in a different style. Unfortunately all the offices went their own ways, starting the date letter cycles at different times, using different alphabets and sometimes missing out some of the letters. I or J were frequently omitted to avoid confusion. Some people, by using mnemonics, manage to keep the date letter systems in their heads, but most people depend on the little pocket guides that are available to identify date letters.

MAKERS' MARKS

The maker's mark, consisting of a set of initial letters, was stamped into any ware of gold or silver by the maker before he submitted it to the assay office. Its purpose was to allow the assay office to identify the wares sent to them, but because of the work of Sir Charles James Jackson and others in tracing these marks they have become an invaluable guide to collectors in identifying the work of different makers. Some confusion has resulted, however, from the fact that anyone could register a mark, a merchant or a retailer, whether he actually wrought plate or not, and such people might order pieces from a workshop and then submit them for assaying with their own marks on them. Usually the maker's mark is the only mark to be found on English gold and silver boxes made in the eighteenth century.

THE DUTY MARKS

It was the practice of the governments of many countries to raise money, from those who could afford such things, by imposing a duty on gold and silver wares. In England between 1720 and 1758 a duty of 6 pence an ounce was levied on silverwares, but the duty was often dodged. To curb this tax avoidance, a duty mark was applied to wares which had paid the tax when the duty was reintroduced in 1784. This duty mark, which continued in use up to 1890, depicted the profile of the reigning sovereign.

SCOTTISH HALLMARKS

Two assay offices in Scotland marked gold and silver; one in Edinburgh and one in Glasgow. These offices used different quality marks from those used in England. From 1759 onwards a thistle mark was added by Edinburgh as a quality mark, to the three-towered castle which had up to that time done duty both as town and quality mark combined. When the new standard for gold was introduced at the end of the eighteenth century, gold wares were marked with a thistle and the figure 18 showing the carat quality. Later 22 carat was marked the same way. The marks for the lower carat qualities were the same as those used in England, and silver continued to be marked with a thistle quality mark.

Throughout the eighteenth century Glasgow used a combined town and quality mark, the complicated city arms consisting of a tree, a bird, a bell, a fish and a ring. Then early in the nineteenth century Glasgow added a rampant lion quality mark, and in the present century added also a thistle mark.

Both the Scottish offices employed a date letter system throughout the eighteenth and nineteenth centuries.

IRISH MARKS

Before 1729 the Dublin assay office used a crowned lamp mark, a maker's mark and sometimes a date letter, but the marking of plate was voluntary in Ireland up to this time. After 1729 Dublin adopted the seated figure of Hibernia as a town mark. Up to 1784 the minimum standard for gold was 22 carat and the Dublin mark for this was a crowned lamp. After 1784 20 carat and 18 carat were legalised and these were marked with a plume of three feathers and unicorn's head erased respectively. The 15, 12 and 9 carat standards legalised after 1854 were marked in the same way as the lower standards in England, that is with the carat quality and the fineness of the silver expressed in parts per thousand. After 1729 the crowned lamp mark was also used to denote sterling silver. Some of the other Irish towns marked silver from time to time, but as no snuff boxes are known bearing provincial Irish marks the collector does not have to concern himself with these.

CHAPTER FOUR

SUBSTITUTES FOR GOLD AND SILVER
IN ENGLAND

As the English middle classes grew prosperous they became, as prosperous people do, acquisitive. One thing these merchants and shopkeepers and their wives wanted to acquire above all else were those status symbols recognised by the establishment of the day. Among other things they coveted the exquisite gold snuff boxes that a Duke, a Lord or a Minister might order from Paris, or from his goldsmith in London. However, even if some merchants could aspire to such things, most of the *nouveau riche* were still not quite wealthy enough to do so. Consequently a demand was created for plausible substitutes that might, in the half light of evening at Vauxhall or Ranelagh Gardens, pass for the real thing. It was to cater for this demand that a Fleet Street watchmaker, Christopher Pinchbeck, evolved and offered to the public in the 1720s a copper alloy that looked very much like the 22 carat gold from which the best snuff boxes of the day were fashioned. The demand for things which looked more precious than they were also motivated Thomas Bolsover to invent Sheffield plate in 1742. He bonded a small block of silver on to a large block of copper by wiring them together and heating them in a furnace. Then he rolled this bimetallic block down between polished rolls to form a brightly polished silver-surfaced sheet. From this could be fabricated a snuff box that would closely resemble a hand-raised silver one.

It was, of course, this demand of the middle classes for possessions and more possessions which led ambitious craftsmen to found factories, to mechanise the processes of manufacture, and so to bring about the Industrial Revolution. It was the huddling together of these stygian factories which turned erstwhile villages such as Birmingham into prosperous if far from beautiful towns. And it was in the new industrial centre of Birmingham, and in nearby Bilston and Wednesbury, that one of the most fascinating of eighteenth-century industries was founded and flourished. Here were produced hundreds of thousands of those charming painted and printed enamel box wares which the late Queen Mary collected so assiduously.

PAINTED AND PRINTED ENAMELS

The snuff boxes produced in the South Staffordshire factories varied greatly in quality. Some of them are very sorry substitutes for the exquisite enamel boxes of Paris, and even at their best they are very provincial. They found a ready sale, however, not only in England but all over the continent as well, despite the fact that there was also a thriving painted enamel industry in the eighteenth century in Germany to compete with the English makers.

The magic name of Battersea has overshadowed the achievements of the South Staffordshire factories. Though it is probably no longer as necessary as it was a few years ago to stress the fly-by-night nature of the York House enterprise which Stephen Theodore Janssen started in 1753, there are still many people who, when shown an English enamel, still ask hopefully—"Is it Battersea?" The extent of the Battersea myth may be judged from the fact that in 1924 it was found that three-quarters of the 400 enamels attributed to Battersea in the famous Schreiber Collection had been made elsewhere. Also in their excellent book on enamels, Therle and Bernard Hughes could state that "Of some seventy examples noted in one day displayed in London and labelled Battersea, not a single piece could have been made there."[1]

The attribution and dating of English enamel boxes is an inexact science to say the least. The makers did not mark their work as did the porcelain manufacturers, and the situation is confused too by the fact that when an enameller closed his business he would sell his unfinished work to his fellow craftsmen. An advertisement for the auction which was held following Janssen's bankruptcy is interesting in this context. Besides the unsold stock—"beautiful enamell'd pictures, snuff boxes, watchcase . . ." there was also included in this sale a "great variety of blank enamels of various sizes, copper frames for mounting the unfinished enamels . . . also a great number of copper plates,

[1] Hughes, Therle and Bernard, *English Painted Enamels*, London, 1951.

84

beautifully engraved by the best hands . . ." With these blank enamels and printing plates a Staffordshire enameller could produce printed enamel boxes identical to ones produced at Battersea. As craftsmen are great ones for putting aside such things for the right occasion, the man who acquired these bits and pieces might well not have turned them into snuff boxes and offered them for sale until perhaps ten or twenty years later.

The colour of the ground on which the printing or painting was applied helps to date painted enamel snuff boxes, though the experts are not unanimous about the probable dates on which the various coloured grounds were first used. Many of Lady Schreiber's four hundred "Battersea" enamels had coloured grounds, and when the collection was recatalogued in 1924 this was one of the bases on which a lot of them were considered to have been wrongly attributed. It was not considered likely, on the evidence provided by contemporary porcelain, that any ground other than white and possibly yellow would have been used before the 1760s, that is at least four or five years after the Battersea factory ceased to produce enamelwares.

Therle and Bernard Hughes have produced a list of presumptive dates for the introduction of the various ground colours, based on their contention that the enamellers probably followed the lead of the Chelsea porcelain factory, which in turn was influenced by developments at the famous French porcelain factory established by Louis XIV at Sèvres. They suggest that the dark blue ground could have been used as early as 1755, and point out that a pea-green ground was mentioned in catalogues in 1757, which, if they are right, means that the Battersea factory could have used either of these. They date the introduction of the yellow ground as 1770, the same date as the pretty rose pompadour ground first used at Sèvres made its appearance on English porcelain.

But is the evidence based on borrowings from Sèvres valid? We know that in the early days the best enamels came from Italy and it is interesting that in 1765 the Society of Arts offered two prizes, one for a white "equal in colour, and all the other properties to the Venetian", the other for "the finest true red colour". So it would seem that in the early days it would have been the colours available from Italy rather than the lead given by the Sèvres porcelains which would have limited the ground colour.

It is, incidentally, significant perhaps that in 1765, the Society of Arts should set store by the need to produce locally a fine and lustrous white, suggesting that this remained the traditional base at this date.

Another indication of late date are the gilt enrichments that were applied increasingly to South Staffordshire enamels. Early examples of these are rare, and when they do exist there is usually little trace left of the original gilding, because before an improved technique was evolved in the middle sixties, the adhesion of the gold leaf or powdered gold was poor. The existence of bright gilt scrolls on a supposed Battersea box would therefore make the attribution improbable.

Mounts were invariably used round the edges of enamelled boxes before the dipping process came to be employed late in the eighteenth century. Before this the enamel was applied with a palette knife, or a brush, and the adhesion round the edges was poor and mounts had to be employed. These mounts were usually made up from copper strip which was then gilded, though Pinchbeck and other alloys were also sometimes used. The early mounts were usually plain ones with very little applied decoration, if any at all. Subtly shaped and decorative mounts indicate post-Battersea work.

The style of painting, too, is a giveaway, at least to those who have handled a considerable number of these boxes. The painting on Battersea boxes tends to ape the French taste, while the South Staffordshire painters often produced work of a naïve English charm. But this is the broadest of generalisations. The enamel painters continued to produce rather unconvincing versions of the popular paintings of Lancret, Watteau and Boucher throughout the century. It is often the minor motifs applied to the sides of a box, which were frequently taken from the pattern books of the period, that help to date it, rather than the more important painting on the lid.

One cannot help wondering why Janssen ever came to start his Battersea factory. He was the wealthy son of a wealthy father. He had been Lord Mayor of London and a City Chamberlain and lived affluently in fashionable Soho Square. Why should such a man risk his fortune in so speculative a venture? He was, we know, very interested in the arts, and it was perhaps this interest which led him to form that fatal partnership with the engraver John Brooks and the pottery manufacturer Henry Delamain, and to set up the factory in York House, a house which he had inherited from his father and which lay conveniently empty. It would seem likely that Brooks and Delamain were convinced that there was a fortune to be made by transferring printed designs on to enamel surfaces instead of laboriously applying the pattern a brush stroke at a time. And presumably they persuaded Janssen to put up the capital for their venture.

If the Battersea factory was far from being a financial success, there is no doubt that it was important in another way. It is almost certain that we owe to the partnership of Janssen, Brooks and Delamain the development of the minor art form of printed enamelling, an art form which remained unique to England, and which gave the country a very healthy export business over the next fifty years. The business which the South Staffordshire enamellers did with France was important enough to cause Napoleon to specifically ban their products and France was far from being the industry's only export market.

The printing technique which was perfected at York House was, incidentally, later applied to porcelain, and is still widely used in the pottery industry to this day.

Painted enamelling applied to small gold wares was a well established craft by the end of the seventeenth century. The English contribution was to make painted enamels available to a wider public by applying the enamel to thin copper sheets, and by turning it into a mass-production industry. This new industry already existed in Birmingham by 1755, by which date John Taylor was employing no fewer than five hundred people to make a variety of small gilt, japanned and enamelled wares. He is said to have employed "one servant" who decorated snuff boxes and "earned £3.10s a week painting them at a farthing each". This one servant was, one would imagine, a master craftsman with a number of journeymen and apprentices working under him. Employing men at such pittance piece rates it is small wonder that, when he died in 1775, John Taylor was worth no less than £200,000.

Though painted enamel snuff boxes might be cheap substitutes for the beautiful Paris boxes, the making of them was nonetheless time consuming and involved many complex processes. The first step was to roll down copper to produce the paper-thin sheet, and to cut out with hammer and punch the pieces from this, which would eventually become the skeleton of the box—lid, sides and base. If the box were of complex shape, and not the more usual oblong, it might be necessary to raise the body and lid with the hammer, though after about 1770 the bodies and lids of boxes were often stamped between dies in a stamping press. The copper surfaces were subsequently scratch-brushed to provide a rough surface to which the enamel would adhere. The copper sheets were then assembled, usually by lap-jointing to form the body and lid.

Meanwhile the white or tinted enamel, which would be used to cover the copper all over on both sides giving it strength as well as providing the sleek surface which would later be decorated by painting or printing, would have been prepared. Enamel is a tough form of glass: broken beer glasses were indeed collected from the pubs of South Staffordshire and used in the making of enamels. The other main constituents of the basic white enamel were lead oxide and tin oxide, the latter being sometimes replaced by arsenic which was cheaper, but must have constituted a considerable hazard to the health of those who worked with it. The coloured enamels were produced by the addition of various metallic oxides, many makers evolving their own variations on the formulae which became closely guarded secrets of the trade.

The ingredients were crushed in mills to a sand-like consistency. This powder was kept covered with water until it was required, and then mixed with oil of lavender and applied to the copper. After this the enamelled copper components were placed in a "coffin", a pipe-clay box designed to protect it from the fumes, and then the enamel was fused in a "muffle" furnace, the oil of lavender which acted only as a medium being driven off by the heat.

The top and bottom of the boxes were now ready for decorating. Painting was done by the artist who applied the coloured enamels to the white or tinted enamel surface, depicting romantic landscapes, classical ruins, flower pieces and portraits of prominent personalities of the day, laboriously adding brush stroke to brush stroke, and firing the piece a number of times between coats. Printed enamelling made it possible to apply a design to the box in one rapid operation, though only rarely was the printed pattern not improved by some overpainting, and sometimes it provided no more than the outline which the painter then filled in.

To produce a printed enamel an engraved copper plate had first to be prepared. The Battersea factory called upon the distinguished engraver, Simon-François Ravenet, among others, to do this work. He "was employed to engrave copper plates from which the articles were stamped, consisting of scrolls, foliage, shells, pastoral subjects and figures of every description". These plates were inked in the same way as engraving plates are inked, the ink used being a compound which would remain stable when heated. Battersea used black, purple, brown and red inks. A sheet of paper was then placed on the plate, and the design pressed on to the paper by passing plate and paper through a mangle. The paper with its inked design was now applied to the snuff box which then went into a muffle where the design was fused into the enamel surface.

One wonders how Janssen's venture came to go bankrupt, producing something for which there was obviously a great demand in England during the middle years of the eighteenth century. Horace Walpole, a man of his time if ever there was one, gave the factory his patronage. He had two pieces of Battersea at least in his collection and sent Richard Bently in 1755 "a trifling snuff box, only as a sample of the new manufacture at Battersea, which is done with copper-plates". Perhaps Janssen costed himself out of the market, employing good artists and paying London rates to his craftsmen, while the South Staffordshire factories paid rates reckoned in pence per day. Things seemed to have gone wrong at York House early in the brief life of the factory. Both Brooks and Delamain withdrew in 1754, and after this Janssen may have ploughed in a great deal of money to keep the firm going, but it has also been suggested that his bankruptcy may have been a personal one, and that the Battersea factory was no more than a contributory factor.

The South Staffordshire factories prospered where Janssen failed. Samuel Yardly, who is believed to have been the first of the Wednesbury enamellers, founded a business in 1776, which

John Yardly, probably his grandson, was still carrying on in 1817. Among the Bilston makers, where the enamelling trade dated back to the 1740s, was Benjamin Bickley who acquired an established enamelling business in 1749. His factory was sold after his son's death in 1776, and the advertisement revealed him as the owner of a large and well-equipped factory standing in eight acres of ground. The equipment included "two mills for grinding enamels". As Therle and Bernard Hughes rightly comment, "The output of this factory must already have been considerable to find use for two grinding mills . . ."[1]

The products of the South Staffordshire enamellers might be described as good, bad and indifferent. At one end of the scale there were boxes like the one from the late Queen Mary's collection which has a rich blue ground with a white diaper pattern enclosing white stars. The painting of a fashionably dressed man and woman in a verdant landscape is surrounded by well-preserved gilded rococo scrolls, which date it as later than 1765. Similar scrolls enclose the painted foliate rose motifs on the sides of the box. At the other end of the scale were the tawdry boxes ill-painted with lifeless landscapes which were mass-produced towards the end of the century.

ENGLISH BASE METAL BOXES

As was mentioned at the beginning of this chapter, two Englishmen, Christopher Pinchbeck and Thomas Bolsover, were responsible for inventing precious metal substitutes early in the eighteenth century, and so providing English snuff-takers of modest means with inexpensive boxes which looked not unlike the gold and silver boxes which wealthier addicts flourished. Copper alloys had been used to make imitation gold jewellery since ancient times, but these were never very convincing. In 1727, however, the London clock and watch maker, Pinchbeck, who specialised in automata and had workshops in Clerkenwell and Fleet Street, devised an alloy consisting of 83 parts of pure rose copper and 17 parts of pure zinc imported from China. He heat-treated this alloy and fabricated watch cases from it that had an appearance very closely resembling those made from gold of the minimum legal standard of 22 carat.

[1] *Ibid*

Besides using his alloy for watch cases Pinchbeck was soon casting jewellery and small wares in it, including snuff boxes made in imitation of the repoussé gold boxes of the day, the cast lids chased up by hand. He also produced bombé boxes, the lids of which were set with polished agates. Even before his death in 1732 inferior copies of his work were beginning to appear, and after his death other makers continued to produce "pinchbeck" wares, usually made of inferior alloys.

Thomas Bolsover's new metal, what we now call "old Sheffield plate", was to be even more commercially successful than Pinchbeck's. Bolsover set up a factory in his native city of Sheffield and produced silver-plated buttons and snuff boxes from his new metal. His invention turned Sheffield into a boom town, and over the next century all manner of wares made from "old Sheffield plate" poured out of the factories there, bringing a new elegance to the middle-class salons and dining rooms of England.

Bolsover produced shallow circular boxes with decoration raised on the lids by stamping tools in imitation of repoussé decoration, or with stamped imitations of flat chasing. He also produced boxes with pierced lids depicting classical scenes and backed with translucent glass. The metal from which these snuff boxes were made only had silver on the top surface, and to disguise the copper interior and to prevent it being tarnished by the snuff, a silver liner was usually fitted to the boxes. Alternatively the copper interior was gilded in the same way that the interiors of silver boxes were invariably gilded at this period. Some Bolsover boxes are also found with tortoise-shell liners.

From 1760 other Sheffield and Birmingham makers, Matthew Boulton among the latter, began to produce oblong boxes from Bolsover's silver-plated sheet. These proved in use to wear badly on the edges, the copper beneath the silver soon showing through. So Matthew Boulton began to sweat silver edges on to his boxes to prevent this and in the latter part of the century other makers followed his example. These edges made it possible to use the fashionable bright-cut decoration on these boxes in the 1780s. If engraved crests were called for it was necessary to solder silver insets into the lids of the boxes, as engraving of the plate would have cut through the silver layer to the copper underneath. The presence of such silver mounts, however, would date a box after about 1810, when this technique was first employed.

In the 1770s snuff boxes were also made from base metal silver substitutes. James Vickers of Sheffield devised a number of tin alloys containing antimony, copper and bismuth which were variously known as "white metal", "Vickers' metal" or later "Britannia metal", after Britannia Place, Sheffield, where they were made, which address was incidentally sometimes inscribed on the boxes made after 1837.

From the end of the seventeenth century references exist to brass snuff boxes, both gilded and left in their natural state. "A Brass Snuff Box gilt with Gold, Engraven on the Lid with the Story of Joseph and Potiphar's Wife" is mentioned in the *London Gazette* in 1692. Plain oval and oblong brass boxes were made in the second half of the eighteenth century, and then in the 1790s snuff boxes were stamped out of brass and gilded. These later boxes had raised decoration imparted to the metal by the tools, and this was chased up by hand before gilding.

Snuff boxes were also made from pewter, and Sir Joshua Reynolds owned a snuff box of "vile and shabby tin". This description of Reynolds's box by Fanny Burney fits all surviving eighteenth-century pewter snuff boxes, oval, oblong, plain or chased. They all have a leaden hue and are for the most part indifferently made. Both brass and pewter snuff boxes were also made on the continent and the dating of these and the attribution of them to any particular country are often quite impossible.

ENGLISH POTTERY AND PORCELAIN BOXES

Most of the eighteenth-century ceramic snuff boxes were made in Germany and France. The soft paste porcelains used in England by the Chelsea Factory of Bow and at Derby were not suitable, not having sufficient strength for boxmaking. Those few pottery snuff boxes that were made in England before 1770 were not particularly distinguished ones.

In the 1740s agateware snuff boxes were produced in Staffordshire by Thomas Whieldon. He made his agateware by stacking slabs of different coloured clays one on top of another and then beating them together. When the stack was then sliced, an effect not dissimilar to the striations of a banded agate was revealed.

This parti-coloured material was subsequently moulded to form the lids and bodies of snuff boxes, and a liquid glaze was applied before the final firing to give the pottery a smooth, non-porous surface. The parts of the boxes were then despatched to Birmingham and Wolverhampton where metal mounts were fitted to them, and they were then assembled. At the Leeds pottery in the 1760s some snuff boxes were produced with screw lids, while a few boxes with blue decoration were made in Bristol.

Then in the 1770s Josiah Wedgwood began to make jasperware snuff boxes. Jasperware is a close-textured stoneware called after the variously coloured silica mineral jasper which Wedgwood sought to imitate. Indeed in 1776 he was to claim that "we are now absolute with jasper". The early boxes are usually inscribed with the names of Wedgwood himself and his partner Bentley. The later ones have only the Wedgwood name on them. Wedgwood snuff boxes are seldom seen nowadays, and not a great many of them can have survived the hard usage which a snuff box tends to suffer. What one does see more often are snuff boxes with Wedgwood panels inserted in the lids. A number of box makers, Matthew Boulton among them, bought these plaques in and set them "in gold and cut steel mountings for snuff boxes".

Popular among these plaques were the "heads of illustrious moderns", 229 of them in all, the best of which were the work of John Flaxman. Flaxman was a fine sculptor and he also produced more imaginative reliefs for the Wedgwood factory, the finest of which, perhaps, was The Muses Watering Pegasus in Helican, used on a surviving circular table snuff box. Flaxman was, it seems, not above doing humbler chores for the factory, for in 1783 he sent Wedgwood a bill for fifteen shillings for "grinding the edges of six snuff boxes".

Some jasperware boxes were also produced in the late 1780s by a rival of Wedgwood, a former pupil of his called William Adam who set up in business for himself in 1769. He also signed his boxes with his surname as Wedgwood did.

ENGLISH JAPANNED IRON BOXES AND PAPIER MÂCHÉ
Besides producing and exporting large numbers of painted enamel boxes, Britain catered for snuffers of modest means at home and abroad by producing many thousands of japanned iron snuff

boxes during the eighteenth century. These were made in a number of different towns, at Sheffield, Birmingham and Wolverhampton, Bilston in Staffordshire and Pontypool and Usk in South Wales. The manufacture of japanned iron boxes had begun at Sheffield and Bilston by the beginning of the century. From 1702 onwards, in the Parish register which recorded the births in the parish of Bilston, some of the fathers of the children were described as "makers of snuff boxes", others as "decorators of snuff boxes". These men worked in the local "snuff houses", that sold their wares for only threepence each. Today these Bilston boxes, made from sheet iron covered with coats of sleek black japan, are rare, and, it must be said, also rather uninspiring objects.

The Welsh boxes, which date from 1720 onwards, were better made, more expensive and more highly regarded by the public of the period. The Pontypool factory is also said to have enjoyed a considerable export business with Holland. This is a little odd because the Dutch were less interested in snuff than any of their continental neighbours. Perhaps the Amsterdam merchants in the gabled houses along the canals re-exported them. Or were the boxes that were sent to Holland in fact tobacco boxes?

The making of japanned iron boxes spread from Bilston to Wolverhampton, also about 1720, but it was not until the 1730s that the Birmingham factories began to produce them. William Hutton, the historian, records that it was to John Taylor, who had a finger in so many pies, that "we owe . . . the japanned and gilt snuff boxes". About the same time, however, another Birmingham man, John Baskerville, also set up a factory for producing them.

It had been the importation of lacquer wares from Japan and China in the seventeenth century which had created interest in producing lacquer substitutes in Europe. Imports of eastern lacquer wares were limited because the process of production was slow and because Japan restricted the export of them. In 1688, two Englishmen, John Stalker and George Parker, published *A Treatise of Japanning, Varnishing and Guilding* which contained a formula for japan based on shellac, which consists of a resin secreted by an insect, combined with paint and alcohol. And it was presumably some such concoction as this which the Bilston and Sheffield makers applied to their iron snuff boxes a decade later.

The Pontypool boxes, which were made at the ironworks of the Hanbury family, resulted from the experiments of Thomas Allgood, who evolved a lacquer consisting of linseed oil, asphaltums and umber. Major John Hanbury who was in charge of the works also dipped his iron in Cornish tin, and then stored it so that the tin penetrated the iron, turning it a silvery colour. This presumably provided a less porous surface to receive the coats of the japan, and therefore produced a better finish.

The earliest japanned boxes were black, but as time went on customers were given a range of colours to choose from. By 1741 Pontypool was already offering the alternative of crimson, and a little later produced a finish that simulated the fashionable and expensive tortoise-shell. By the 1760s and 1770s both Pontypool and Birmingham were offering japanned boxes in a wide range of shapes. Pontypool made them in tomato red, dark green, bright blue and canary yellow, orange and puce and grey. The Birmingham and Wolverhampton colour range was similar, but also included brown and white.

As can be seen from the boxes in the National Museum of Wales at Cardiff, those from the Pontypool factory were usually decorated with the owner's name in gold or some admonition such as "be merry and wise" or "Come smoak, drink chat and be merry with me", this last surely identifying the box on which it appears not as a snuff box but as a tobacco box. It is interesting to note that most of the japanned iron snuff boxes had loose lids. Presumably if one paid only a few pence for one's snuff box one had to suffer some inconvenience. The Pontypool factory also decorated its boxes with "Chinese landscapes and figures in gold . . ." as Richard Pococke observed on his travels in the 1750s. Pococke drew a comparison, too, between the Pontypool factory, which restricted its decoration to painting in gold, and the Birmingham makers who painted their boxes in many colours. The innovator of this multi-colour decoration is believed to have been Taylor's competitor, John Baskerville.

Japanned iron boxes began to lose their popularity in the latter part of the century though production continued at Pontypool and Usk well into the nineteenth century. One of the reasons for the decline in the popularity of these boxes was almost certainly the result of the improvement of papier-mâché boxes at this period.

Papier-mâché snuff boxes were originally made out of either paper or rags. If rags were used they were mixed with glue. If paper was used, this was chewed up (*mâcher* means to chew) and combined with water to produce a mash. This mash could then be moulded to form the bodies and lids of boxes. These moulded shapes were quite hard when dried, and were then japanned, usually black, and decorated with painting and gilding in the same way as the japanned iron boxes. The Birmingham manufacturer John Taylor, who pioneered so many new techniques of boxmaking, may also have been the man to introduce the papier-mâché snuff boxes made in this way, at some date between 1740 and 1750.

The mass production of papier-mâché boxes, which was to become a considerable industry in the nineteenth century, followed the evolution of a different technique of production by another Birmingham man, Henry Clay. His process, which he patented in 1772, consisted of pasting layers of porous glued paper one on top of another in a metal mould, until the required thickness was achieved. Each layer of paper was oven-dried and the completed shape, when removed from the mould, was filed and polished and then japanned. It was as a result of Clay's process that the japanned paper box eventually replaced the japanned iron box in public favour.

CHAPTER FIVE

SNUFFING UTENSILS IN SCOTLAND IN THE EIGHTEENTH CENTURY

Like some Scandinavian snuff-takers, the Scottish snuffer continued to prefer a horn to a box throughout the century. The early Scottish snuff horns date from before 1603 when the English court was intrigued to see James I's Highlanders using them. These horns were sometimes called "snuff mulls", sometimes "Sneeshin miln", and they were indeed mills for the inside of the horn was ridged. A carrot of tobacco leaves, or the leaves of the sneezewort which were preferred in Scotland, could be powdered by twisting it inside the horn. Later when it became the custom to buy the snuff or sneezewort ready-rubbed, the practice of milling the horn ceased and the inside was then polished like the outside.

There are two types of mulls, the Scottish equivalents of the pocket and table snuff boxes of the English. The pocket mulls were made from sheep's horn, and the horn was usually boiled to make it pliable and then twisted into a tight scroll, compact and convenient for the pocket. A lid was provided to plug up the open end of the horn. Made either of horn or of silver, this lid was hinged, and the silver lids were often set with a stone. Usually one of Scotland's native gemstones was used, a faceted rock crystal or the smoky brown quartz found in the Cairngorms and named after the region. Often eighteenth-century mulls had little chains soldered on to the mount, and from these depended two or more accoutrements, a little silver ladle and a hare's foot or brush on a silver mount, used by the owner to sweep any offensive-looking grains away from his nostrils after he had partaken of his snuff, and sometimes a little mallet to dislodge the snuff from the walls of the mull (see plate 20). Besides these pocket mulls, larger table ones were made in considerable numbers from the horns of Highland cattle. The mouth of these horns usually had a silver lid; a silver mount on the tip of the horn, and little silver feet for it to stand on were a feature of many of these table mulls.

CHAPTER SIX

EIGHTEENTH-CENTURY SCANDINAVIAN BOXES

Great numbers of eighteenth-century Scandinavian snuff boxes survive in public and private collections, and numerous paintings and drawings depict Danish, Swedish, Norwegian and Finnish men and women taking snuff or holding snuff boxes. The featuring of snuff boxes in formal portraits of fashionable people makes it apparent that snuffing was, as it was in France, one of the social graces in these northern countries throughout the eighteenth century. There is ample evidence that both Sweden and Denmark supported large numbers of skilled craftsmen capable of forming and decorating beautiful gold and silver boxes, some of them comparable with those produced by the Paris masters. The upper classes in Finland fostered the boxmakers too, but unfortunately most of the boxes which were made there in periods of affluence went into the melting pot in more troubled times. Norway was a less wealthy country than her neighbours, and only Bergen and Trondheim had a privileged minority with the means to patronise gold- and silversmiths, so that Norwegian gold and silver boxes are comparatively rare.

Most of the Scandinavian boxes show the influence of foreign cultures. Some are exact replicas of French, German and English boxes, while many others are local variations on foreign themes. Probably some of the Scandinavian makers were trained in Paris or expatriate craftsmen were employed in their workshops. It seems likely that the Scandinavian boxmakers obtained many of their designs from abroad, and during the rococo period we know that they actually bought in rough repoussé castings from Germany which they chased up and incorporated in the lids of their boxes. However, the Scandinavian makers did not only slavishly copy the motifs fashionable elsewhere. In the rococo period some of them showed originality in their interpretation of the mannerisms of this fashion, which incidentally lingered there as late as the 1770s. Sometimes, too, the Scandinavian chasers and engravers introduced characteristic local details into their designs, and even now and again the boxmakers of Denmark, Sweden and Norway produced local forms not found elsewhere.

SCANDINAVIAN GOLD BOXES

The finest gold boxes to survive are the work of Swedish makers, though some fine gold boxes made by Danish and Norwegian craftsmen can be found. Many of these gold boxes are second-rate provincial copies of Paris models. A few, like those from the workshops of Frantz Bergs in Stockholm and the Fabritius family, who worked in Copenhagen from 1708 until well into the nineteenth century, are comparable to anything made in Paris. Frantz Bergs's boxes, made in the 1750s and 1760s, are in the rococo style. The best of them are those decorated with repoussé chasing. When he used enamel decoration as a result of the demands of fashion or his own inclinations, it would seem that he could not command the services of a really fine enameller. There were chasers in plenty, however, who were capable of quite superb work, for it is obvious from inspecting his boxes that his chasing was carried out by a number of different craftsmen. Take for example the round box made about 1760, now in a Swedish private collection. This shows a seated female figure in a surround of rococo scrolls, shells, fruit and flowers. The detail is not particularly sharp but rounded and softly outlined, similar to that seen on many Scandinavian silver boxes of the period. Different from this is the chasing on one of Bergs's typical baroque form boxes now in the Nationalmuseet in Stockholm (plate 21). This must be one of the finest examples of chasing on the small scale to be produced anywhere in the eighteenth century. The delineation of the allegorical scene in the rococo cartouche on the lid, of the enclosing scrolls, and of the matting and scalework, is of an incredible delicacy. The shell and scroll design on the base is a small masterpiece of composition, and the walls of the box have fine elongated, lobbed work that is a characteristic of Bergs's boxes but is also to be seen on a larger scale on the bodies of many eighteenth-century Scandinavian silver vessels.

There is another baroque-shaped box of Bergs's, sold by

Sotheby's in London in 1964, that was almost certainly decorated by this same chaser, but it is inconceivable that he also decorated two of Bergs's boxes now in Swedish private collections. The man who chased these was also a fine artist with hammer and chisel, but the style of his chasing is as different from that on the box in the Nationalmuseet as a painting by Watteau is different from one by Teniers. Both these boxes, made about 1760, are oblong, and the repoussé chasing is so vigorous that it looks as though the boxes were encrusted with decoration. Within the inevitable rococo scrollwork frame, one depicts a stag at bay, the hounds sinking their fangs into the flesh of the animal and the huntsman, astride a prancing horse, blowing his horn to call them off. In the background a bold pattern of chased ripplework suggests a gathering storm. The other box, again decorated by a different hand, is overall chased with an incrustation of repoussé shellwork scattered with fruit and flowers. A very similar Bergs box, made in 1753, belongs to the Swedish royal family. This is further enriched by a thumbpiece set with diamonds, emeralds and rubies.

If the enamel painting on Bergs's oblong and oval boxes is usually rather second-rate, this cannot be said of a shaped box which his workshop produced in about 1760 and which now belongs to Professor Frosterus of Helsinki. This is decorated all over with cloisonné arabesques of flowers and foliage, very similar in style to the decorations used on watch cases, miniature cases and lockets made a hundred and fifty years earlier in France and England. This box is quite as beautiful, quite as original and quite as accomplished as any made in Paris at this time.

Frantz Bergs was not, of course, the only maker of Swedish gold boxes. In the 1750s and 1760s Andreas Almgren made some oblong enamel boxes decorated with *basse-taille* enamel figure groups of the type currently popular in France, and in 1763 Anders Liedberg produced a deep oblong box with flower sprays at the centre of engraved sunbursts, reminiscent of that beautiful box by Barnabé Sageret in the Louvre, though Sageret's box with its enamelled flowers is more colourful than Liedberg's box, on which naturalistic flowers are chased up in gold.

There exist, too, a considerable number of Swedish gold boxes in the Louis Seize style, produced from 1768 onwards. These are generally rather inferior to the French models on which they were based. An exceptionally fine box, now in an American private collection, was produced, however, by Friedrich Fyrwald of Stockholm about 1770. The unenamelled areas are in *quatre-couleur* gold. The medallion in the centre of the lid is a miniature portrait enclosed in areas of enamel, and the lid is further enriched with a scattering of diamonds. The walls of the box have areas of enamel enclosing small oval medallions between chased neo-classical motifs. Fyrwald also produced a number of little oval boxes in a style which seems to have been very popular at this time, decorated with engine-turning scattered with pearl motifs, and covered with transparent enamelling. Kenneth Snowman also illustrates a fine box usually attributed to Fyrwald, at one time in the Hermitage collection. This was a *grisaille* portrait of Catherine the Great on the lid in a surround decorated with diamonds and enamel. Other Stockholm makers who produced gold boxes at this time were Carl Lundberg, Anders Zachoun, Mikael Astrom and Peter Johan Ljungstedt.

The Danish makers of the 1760s also produced some outstanding gold boxes. There are two very attractive *en cage* boxes from this period, the bodies carved from amethyst, one of them by Christopher Fabritius. This maker also produced, in 1758, a well shaped oblong box decorated with rococo repoussé chasing of allegorical and architectural motifs, and a round box with a miniature painted enamel in the manner of Teniers on the lid, surrounded by a wreath of *basse-taille* flowers and leaves. Perhaps the prettiest gold box of the rococo period was the work of Jacob Henrichsen Möinichen of Copenhagen. He made this oblong box in 1758, and had it decorated with *basse-taille* and painted enamel sprays of colourful flowers tied with blue ribbon bows against an engraved chequerboard ground.

Another of the Fabritius family, Frederick the younger, was responsible for a magnificent *en cage* box, which he made about 1770 and which is now in the Kunstindustrimuseet at Copenhagen. This box consists of a series of moss agates in a chased *quatre-couleur* frame. The motifs, which the chaser has chiselled into this frame, consist of scrolled trellises delicately scattered with flowers. There is a very similar moss agate *en cage* box at Temple Newsam

House in the style of James Cox and believed to be of English make. This English box is, however, very pedestrian compared with the Fabritius box. The maker of the box at Temple Newsam obviously had little feeling for the rococo, and only pays lip service to the mannerisms of the style. Frederick Fabritius, on the other hand, has contained within the straight edges of his oblong box a riot of line and adventurous composition that is rococo at its best. He has produced not just a fine piece of craftsmanship but a work of art in gold and gemstones.

Frederick Fabritius went on to adapt to Louis Seize style in the 1780s and some pretty little oval boxes were produced in his workshop, but they show little originality and might have been produced anywhere in Europe in the last quarter of the eighteenth century.

The Norwegian smallworkers also produced a few gold boxes, but they are for the most part rather undistinguished gold versions of silver boxes. There is, however, a rather fine little baroque-form box in the Vestlandske Kunstindustmuseum at Bergen made in 1745 by Michael Hansen Blytt, well chased on the complex little lid with scrollwork and with a little miniature portrait on the inside. Blytt was better known as a maker of rococo silver boxes, and this is the only known example of his work in gold.

THE SILVER BOXES OF SCANDINAVIA

If Scandinavian gold boxes are rare the same cannot be said of silver boxes. Probably more eighteenth-century Danish, Swedish and Norwegian silver boxes have come down to us than we have inherited from any other area of Europe. There are a number of boxes dating from as early as the first decade of the century, but the great period of silver snuff box making was the rococo period. The fashion for rococo lasted for thirty-five years or more in Scandinavia, from about 1740 to as late as 1775, and hundreds of boxes in this style still exist, attesting to dozens of makers' taste and skill in handling this demanding style.

The earliest existing Danish silver box which could conceivably have been used for snuff, is a shallow disc-form box of about 1670. It has a removable flat lid engraved with a crowned monogram in a surround of scrolled acanthus leaves. A band of similar decoration encircles the walls of the box. Another little round box of Danish origin, with a removable lid decorated with a rosette and made about 1700, also has similar acanthus decoration round the body.

The earliest Danish hinged boxes which were definitely made for snuff date from the period 1700 to 1710. They are shallow oblong boxes, unusual in being hinged on one of the shorter sides of the oblong. One of these boxes, made in 1707, has an engraved crest in a surround of flowers and foliage on the lid, but two others have low-relief repoussé baroque decoration all over their lids, similar to that on French silver boxes from this period.

From this same period we have two Swedish silver boxes of considerable originality. One of these in the Nationalmuseet at Stockholm was made by Petter Bernegau, who worked in the city from 1706 to 1733. On the lid of this oval box there is a lively battle scene with a horseman in the foreground discharging his pistol at another mounted man. The semi-circular rim surrounding this scene is decorated with formal baroque chasing on a matted ground. The other early Swedish box is an oblong one with canted corners in the Nordiska Museet collection. This is flat-chased on the lid with a portrait of Charles XII in an oval, surrounded by foliate work enclosing circular symbolic motifs. On the base similar circles among foliate chasing are engraved with the names and dates of his battles.

From the Regence period which began in 1715, we have many more varied types of snuff boxes. At this time both Danish and Norwegian makers produced silver boxes in the form of books, the tooling on the bindings being simulated by engraving or chasing. An example of 1715 has a decorated spine, two clasps, and chased crests that reproduce those that would have been tooled into the leather binding. Silver book-form boxes seem to be unique to Scandinavia, but wooden book snuff boxes were made elsewhere in Europe from early in the eighteenth century up until the nineteenth century.

At this period the Danish makers produced the first of those baroque-form boxes, which in Scandinavia remained popular until the 1770s. Most of these early shaped boxes were flat-chased or engraved with floral motifs, as were the oblong boxes and the canted-corner oblong boxes made at this time. These boxes were composed of a number of components soldered together, and a shaped box might consist of fourteen components each precisely shaped up from the silver sheet with a hammer over a swaging block. The components were then soldered together to form the body and the lid, and on a well-made box, which many of the Scandinavian boxes were, the solderer used just precisely the right amount of the lower melting point silver solder to produce joints that were all but invisible when they were polished.

The Danish makers of the Regence also produced boxes in fancy shapes. Jens Kieldsen Sommerfeldt made a small shell-shaped box about 1735, very like an English box in the Victoria and Albert Museum collection. This same maker was also responsible for a very tall narrow box with a naïve engraving on the lid depicting a church, a flower and a flock of birds. He provided a little spoon, like a coffee spoon, to ladle the snuff from the depths of this rather impractical little box, which would easily have been knocked over on a table and would not have fitted very conveniently into a pocket.

Most of the Norwegian boxes from this period are very simple. There are plain oblong boxes, undecorated oblong ones with canted corners, and shaped boxes with lids mounted with stones or with mother-of-pearl. Only from about 1740 onwards did the Norwegian makers begin to produce more sophisticated boxes of complex form, fashionably chased.

The Swedish makers continued throughout the Regence to produce mainly shallow rectangular silver boxes with low relief repoussé baroque decoration. These remained fashionable there right up to the time when the rococo fad arrived from France in the 1740s. Even as late as 1750 some Swedish makers continued to produce their shallow rectangular boxes. The Swedish silver box workshops did sometimes, however, make boxes in forms other than oblong in the early decades of the century. There is, for instance, a baroque decorated purse-shaped box in the Kunstindustrimuseet in Copenhagen made in Sweden about 1735, but shaped boxes of this kind dating before 1740 are exceptional.

Almost identical boxes to those produced in Sweden were made in Finland in the 1740s. A typical Finnish box from this period is to be seen in the Nordiska Museet in Stockholm, and there is another in the Röhsska Museet in Göteborg, decorated all over with low-relief baroque imagery against a matted ground. There is also a rather badly worn Finnish box in the National Museum, Helsinki, in this same style.

The best of the Scandinavian silver boxes, both from the point of view of craftsmanship and design, were unquestionably those made in the thirty years after 1740. The lids of these rococo boxes were sometimes repoussé-chased but more often cast-chased, many of the castings being imported, almost certainly from Germany. The same casting was used by different makers in Denmark, Sweden and Norway, being chased up with varying degrees of expertise and incorporated in different shaped lids. Bo Bramsen, in his definitive study of Scandinavian snuff boxes,[1] illustrates the same Mars and Venus casting incorporated in boxes by two different Copenhagen makers. Gerhard Hass used it on an oblong box he made in 1753, and three years later Bendix Christensen incorporated it in the lid of a shaped box to greater effect. Another casting depicting a woman, probably intended to be Venus reclining in a shell among rococo scrollwork, was used time and time again. It appears on the lids of two round Swedish boxes of 1760, with minor variations resulting from the chasing. In the same year a Norwegian maker used it for a shaped box as did a Danish and a German maker. It appears too on a shaped Swedish box of about the same period, and another Swedish maker must have had one of these castings lying around in his workshop for a long time for he incorporated it in a shaped box as late as 1777, long after the Louis Seize style had ousted the rococo from popular favour.

The chasers of Scandinavia often reverted to themes popular elsewhere in Europe, perhaps copying them out of pattern books, as has been suggested earlier. A very popular allegory of the middle years of the eighteenth century was Hercules at the cross-roads, usually renouncing Venus in favour of Minerva. This is depicted by an unknown chaser on a silver box made by Hendrich Dysterdijk in 1744. Another chaser produced the figures in identical postures on a Swedish box of about 1760. Again the figures on an English gold box of about 1740 in the Victoria and Albert Museum would seem to have been taken from the same original. On the other hand, a Dutch box in the collection of Karel Citroen (illustrated in plate 22) shows that the chaser has

[1] Bramsen, *op. cit.*

taken liberties with tradition. On this box Hercules appears to be more interested in love and disinclined to embrace reason.

The chasers responsible for decorating the Scandinavian rococo boxes did not invariably copy foreign designs; instead they would give the boxes a local colour. On the lid of one Danish rococo box, for instance, there is depicted a swan's nest among trees, and on another a fruit-picking scene. On a Swedish box of 1745 there is a delightfully naïve interpretation of Noah and his ark safely landed on Mount Ararat. Local churches pop up in the midst of worldly scrollwork, perhaps added by the local engraver to please the owner of the box. But for the most part, the rococo decoration was what it was everywhere. There were the allegorical figure groups, the scenes of dalliance and occasionally there were chinoiseries. And around these little pictures in repoussé run borders of ebullience, riots of scrolls and shells, fruit and flowers. It was a strange, rather over-ripe style, and long before it had run its course in Scandinavia its mannerisms had become vapid gestures. But it was a style admirably suited to the decoration of snuff boxes, its asymmetry giving them a vitality, the wealth of detail providing an enrichment, which because it was in miniature did not become cloying.

Boxes were made in all shapes and all sizes, but there would seem to have been some local preferences in the matter of shape. Most of the Danish boxes are in the most conventional baroque shape, or oblong boxes with outswept walls. The Swedish makers, on the other hand, preferred a round shape. A few round boxes were also made in Norway.

There are too the out-of-style boxes in silver which one finds in every area and in every period. There is, for example, a most unusual Swedish double box, made by C. Älännings of Stockholm in 1759 in the form of a square canister with lids top and bottom, with all the surfaces decorated in engraved rose sprays against a diapered ground. Then there are the trunk-shaped boxes with horticultural trophies from which sunbursts explode, borrowed from French originals and looking rather provincial in their silver form, and not very expertly engraved. Then from Denmark there is a form box representing a seated bird, made about 1750. And there is a delightful little deep oblong box, made in Norway about 1760, now in the Kunstindustrimuseet in Oslo. This is made of wood, but has applied pierced silver decoration on the lid. This piercing depicts scenes of rustic gallantry, the fond couples and some accompanying domestic animals being framed in the curves of wandering asymmetric scrollwork, a charming fusion of rural imagery and metropolitan fashion. And then of course there are the silver-mounted cowrie shells that were as popular as snuff boxes over a long period in Scandinavia as they were elsewhere. There is a Danish one made as early as 1750, unusual for having the hinge at the side instead of at the wider end of the heart-shaped shell. A Norwegian example of about 1770 is also side-hinged. Lars Berg of Copenhagen in 1760 applied artistic logic, by providing the spotted shell with an ornate rococo lid, deeply repoussé-chased with a Venus among shells and scrolls. The result is a piling of Pelion on shady Olympus. Most makers in Scandinavia, in England and in America instinctively provided these shells with simple lids, decorated with restrained engraved or chased decoration. And how much more effective is this simplicity.

Some Scandinavian silversmiths imitated the form of these shell boxes in silver. About 1770 the Norwegian Daniel Irichsen Schebs produced a shell form box with an elaborately flat-chased lid in the rococo style, the silver body decorated with repoussé spoon handle motifs. In about 1780 a Danish maker made a similar box with an elaborately chased lid hinged on the top.

Considerable numbers of silver boxes were made in the Louis Seize style in Sweden, Denmark and Norway, between 1770 and 1800. These oval boxes, lacking the colour imparted to them by enamelling, never seem to be completely successful. Some of the Scandinavian makers did their best to make up for the lack of colour by the elaborateness of the engraving and chasing applied to lid and sides. In most cases this decoration is in the neo-classic tradition, with the inevitable medallion motif on the lid, the decorative surround and the architectural motifs on the walls of the box. Strangely enough the least happy of these boxes are just those where the chaser or engraver has tried to substitute all-over hatching for the enamelled engine-turned panels of the gold originals from Paris which inspired those silver copies. A box made by Daniel Lindstrom in 1781, now in the Nordiska Museet in Stockholm, is a good example of this over-engraving, while a box made the following year by the Danish maker,

Andreas Holm, now in the Kunstindustrimuseet in Copenhagen, shows how much more effective a delicate suggestion of the neo-classical was than an overabundance of it.

In the 1780s the Danish boxmakers also produced some neo-classical boxes of casket form, deep oblong boxes with rounded ends. All that can be said of these was that the application to them of Louis Seize decoration presented almost insuperable problems, and only on one of these, which was made by the Copenhagen maker Lars Olsen in 1785 with borders of reed and ribbon decoration, and with an applied initial on the lid, has the marriage been happily achieved.

In the 1750s and 1760s Denmark produced some painted enamel snuff boxes, very similar in style to those produced in England and Germany at this time. The Royal Copenhagen porcelain factory also produced some fine ceramic snuff boxes between 1775 and the end of the century, but as only three hundred of these boxes were produced all told, they are very rare. The Kunstindustrimuseet in Copenhagen has a fine collection of them, including a charming box made in the 1780s decorated with a basket-weave pattern interspersed with medallions. In the museum there is also a little oval box of the same period with cupids and rosebuds delicately painted in pastel colours on the outside, and inside the lid there is a miniature painting of a doting couple with their offspring. Others are decorated with conventional floral posies and landscapes.

In this same museum and in the Nationalmuseet in Stockholm one can see two examples of Swedish faience boxes made at Marieberg and Rörstrand in the 1760s and 1770s. Again floral motifs and landscapes are the most usual decoration found on the productions of these two potteries, though there is in the Copenhagen museum one with a portrait of Gustav III in profile on the lid.

In Scandinavia, as in all the countries where snuff was taken, boxes were made in more mundane materials than gold or silver, fine porcelain and faience. There are in existence Scandinavian snuff boxes made from brass and from pewter, from wood, horn and bone, over a period of some two centuries.

CHAPTER SEVEN

GERMAN EIGHTEENTH-CENTURY BOXES

No part of Europe produced snuff containers in greater variety than the collection of kingdoms and principalities that comprised the Germany of the eighteenth century. The finest of all the porcelain boxes were produced at the Meissen factory, first under the direction of Johann Friedrich Böttger, then under an avid collector of snuff boxes, Count Heinrich von Brühl, and finally, after the Prussian army occupied Dresden during the Seven Years War, under the patronage of Frederick the Great. In the Saxon capital Heinrich Taddel evolved the *zellenmosaik* box, and his apprentices Johann Christian Neuber and Christian Gottlieb Stiehl carried on the tradition, producing the type of box which Mrs Piozzi described in 1786 as

> consisting of various gems, none bigger than a barley-corn, each of prodigious value, and the workmanship of more, every square being inlaid so neatly, and no precious stone repeated, though the number is no less than one hundred and eighty-three . . . [See plate 23.]

Frederick the Great also established a box-making industry in Berlin, and persuaded distinguished foreign craftsmen to settle there. He supervised the design and production of those opulent, over-loaded table snuff boxes that he gave as diplomatic presents or added to his own collection, which by the time he died numbered some 1,500 boxes.

The earliest surviving German snuff containers are the flasks of ivory, horn and wood dating from the second half of the seventeenth century. The earliest extant boxes are oval ones of horn or ivory, their lids decorated with pressed or carved allegories in relief dating from the period 1690 to 1710. Silver boxes exist dating from the second decade of the eighteenth century, closely resembling the Scandinavian and French boxes of the period.

The earliest ones had lids chased in low relief or flat-chased. Later examples of baroque form were decorated with repoussé-chased or cast-chased rococo decoration, and as has already been mentioned, the Scandinavian makers used rococo castings obtained from German workshops.

The "wearing" of snuff boxes was restricted by sumptuary decree in many areas of Germany to the privileged few, and most of the gold snuff boxes owned by the aristocracy who were permitted to use them came from Paris. In 1740, however, Frederick the Great forbade the importation of gold snuff boxes and other jewels from France into the areas he controlled, with the object of stimulating the development of local craft workshops.

A few early eighteenth-century German gold and *en cage* boxes exist, some of them from perhaps as early as the 1730s. It is difficult, though, to date German boxes accurately or to be sure of where they were made, as they bear no marks, except perhaps the signature of the maker. These early boxes are French in style, and it is only after about 1740 that the boxes made in Dresden and elsewhere become distinctively Germanic. We see the beginnings of this German style in the early work of Heinrich Taddel, who became a master goldsmith in 1739 and produced some extraordinarily lavish rock crystal *en cage* snuff boxes shortly after that date. The gold mounts on these are not just more elaborate than French work but more ponderous, and the scrollwork is set with diamonds which only serve to emphasise their clumsiness. Almost all German boxes are pompous rather than elegant.

Where the German genius lay was in the use of gemstones and decorative minerals. In Dresden in the middle years of the eighteenth century, some very rich *en cage* boxes were produced out of carved rock crystal and other quartz minerals. From this period too came those rather ridiculous Dresden animal boxes, a collection of which can be seen in the Hermitage in Leningrad. There are those grinning lions carved from agate, with diamond-set teeth and eyes. And there is a stag with a rather pained expression, also with diamond teeth and eyes, its antlers and hooves trimmed with diamonds and its lolling tongue carved from ruby. The plinths on which these animals lie form the boxes with hinged lids fitted in the bases.

At the same period the Berlin makers were encrusting their gold boxes with relief mosaics, scenes composed of little pieces of tinted mother-of-pearl and ivory, amethyst and chalcedony. A superb example of this work, from a later period, is a box made in Berlin about 1760. The illustration on plate 24 shows only two sides of this box, but every surface of it has domestic scenes from high life applied to the red-gold body of the box, while the gold itself is richly chased and engraved with architectural motifs. The box is also supplied with a thumbpiece lavishly set with diamonds, a feature characteristic of Berlin boxes from the 1730s onwards.

Some amusing *en cage* boxes, usually attributed to the Dresden makers, the Hoffmanns, were produced in the third quarter of the century. The panels of these boxes consisted of translucent quartz, to which insects and flowers carved from a variety of minerals were applied, the legs and antenna of the insects being engraved on the quartz.

Germany was rich in minerals; virtually every member of the quartz family was being mined in Bohemia, in the area around the twin towns of Idar and Oberstein, where the Romans had found agates, and in Silesia. The boxmaker who exploited this wealth of variously coloured minerals to produce a quite new type of snuff box was Heinrich Taddel. The technique he devised, which was known as *zellenmosaik*, had been first used by the Ancient Egyptians, for what Taddel did in the 1760s was to set gem material cloisonné in the same way that Tutankhamun's jewellers had done thousands of years earlier. On the surfaces of his boxes he built up a pattern of cells, or cloisons, by soldering on pieces of gold strip. He then cut his polished gem materials to fit into the cloisons and rubbed over the top of the gold strip to hold the stones in position. In this way he produced colourful if rather naïve mosaic pictures on the lids, on the bases, and on the walls of his oval boxes. He depicted mainly scenes of village life and birds amongst foliage.

Taddel's apprentice, Johann Christian Neuber, later used the same technique to produce what amounted to gem specimen boxes, known as *Stein Kabinettstabatieren*, or *Cabinet des Pierres*, inlaying the lid and body of a circular or oval box with perhaps 70 or 100 little segments of stone, each one different from the others. Inside the box, as Mrs Piozzi wrote, there would be under "a false bottom besides of gold, opening with a spring touch, . . . a written catalogue of the jewels in the finest handwriting, and the smallest possible". In the centre of the lids of these boxes there was usually a motif in relief mosaic. Some of these medallions depict bouquets of flowers or sometimes they are in the form of portraits. Often these boxes were further enriched with circlets of simulated pearls. Besides the *Stein Kabinett* boxes, Neuber also created more attractive boxes which he decorated with formal patterns of *zellenmosaik*. One has a brick and sunburst pattern in cornelian, mocca stone and agate. On another box using a different technique, he created a basket-work pattern by inlaying, in quartzite panels, different coloured chalcedonies. In the lid of this charming box he also set a floral plaque of Meissen porcelain, which he surrounded with a border of forget-me-nots with turquoise petals and bloodstone leaves, tied with a bow of cornelian.

Other craftsmen exploited the popularity of Neuber's style, chief among them Christian Gottlieb Stiehl. Whereas Neuber's designs tended to formality and symmetry, Stiehl used curved pieces of material to produce asymmetric patterns. He also set his stone *à jour*, that is he dispensed with a backing, so that if his boxes are held up to the light the effect is similar to a stained glass window.

Frederick the Great, that strange man who was at once an aesthete and a remorseless warrior, encouraged foreign artists and craftsmen to work in his Berlin factory. He attracted the talented Pole, Daniel Chodowiecki, an enameller and engraver who subsequently became the King's artistic adviser. He brought the Huguenot goldsmith, Daniel Baudesson, to Berlin to produce boxes there of a Parisian elegance, though somewhat marred by those inevitable Berlin thumbpieces overloaded with diamonds. But for these thumbpieces, Baudesson's boxes, decorated as they usually were with *basse-taille* enamelling, might well have been attributed to some unidentified Parisian goldsmith. The most influential of all the foreign goldsmiths to be attracted to Berlin by Frederick's lavish patronage was undoubtedly Jean Guillaume George Krüger. Krüger was born in London in 1728 though his name leaves little doubt that his parentage was anything but English, and he had studied his craft in Paris before he arrived in Berlin. A comparison of Krüger's surviving designs, with those

14. Unmarked silver box with cabochon agate in lid, mid-eighteenth century, probably Scandinavian but possibly English. James Walker collection.

15. Very fine *piqué posé* work on tortoise-shell, French or English late eighteenth century. James Walker Collection.

16. *Piqué posé* work on the tortoise-shell lid of an old Sheffield plate box, late eighteenth century. James Walker Collection.

17. Silver lid of a late eighteenth century cowrie shell box with a bright-cut border and engraved coat of arms. James Walker Collection.

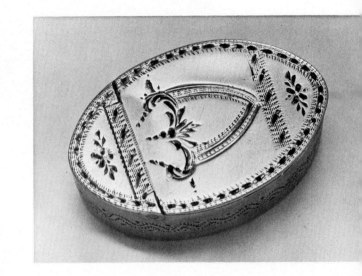

18. An example of Samuel Pemberton's early work in the Louis Seize style with the English top hinge. Silver, hallmarked in 1798. Birmingham Museum.

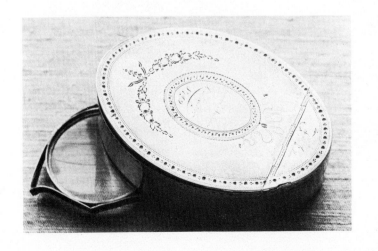

19. Unusual oval box engraved Samuel Nichols, Leominster, 1789 with a hinged magnifying glass that fits in a compartment in the base. James Walker Collection.

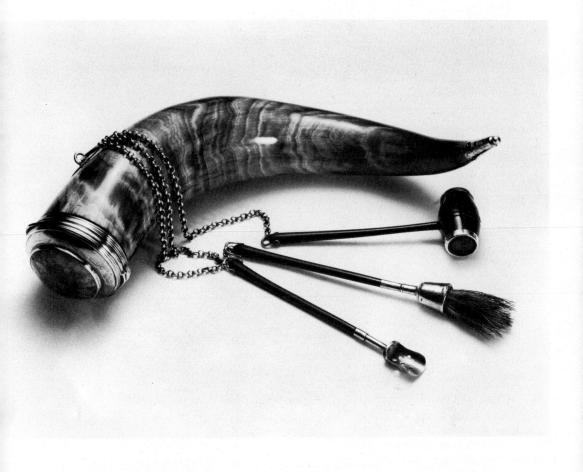

20. A silver-mounted Perth snuff mull with the accoutrements attached by chains. James Walker Collection.

21. Chased gold rococo box made by the great Stockholm box maker, Frantz Bergs in 1773. National Museum, Stockholm.

22. A very interesting gold repoussé box made by Jacques Girardin. This box is unusual in that while the theme – Hercules at the cross roads – was a popular one, here Hercules is turning not as usual towards Minerva but towards Venus. Private Collection, Holland.

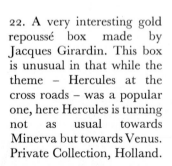

23. Four Dresden *Zellenmosaik* boxes made in the 1760's. Victoria and Albert
Museum.

24. Gold box with panels decorated with tinted shell work. Made in Berlin about 1750. Rijksmuseum, Amsterdam.

25. Outstanding Meissen porcelain box of 1745/50 with gold mounts set with diamonds and rubies. Rijksmuseum, Amsterdam.

26. Earliest known Dutch silver snuff box is this one made about 1667 in the north of the Netherlands, and is obviously the work of a watch-case maker. It is also a very early example of repoussé chasing applied to a box. Rikjsmuseum, Amsterdam.

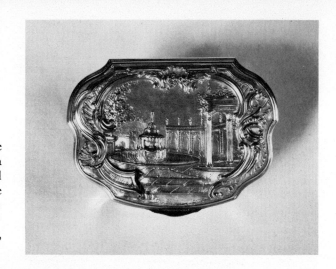

. The finest surviving example of the
ork of the Huguenot goldsmiths in
msterdam. Made by an unidentified
aker with the initials I.S. in 1739. The
asing is comparable to that on Frantz
rgs' boxes from Sweden and the Moser
oxes produced in England. Rijksmuseum,
msterdam.

. Dutch provincial silver snuff box, made
Antony Van der Heul in 1727 in
iddleburg. The ice-scape on the lid is
graved. Rijksmuseum, Amsterdam.

29. Chased New England silver box
made between 1730 and 1740,
possibly by Benjamin Brenton. Courtesy, The Henry Francis du Pont
Winterthur Museum, U.S.A.

30. Deep oblong silver table box with repoussé-chased hunting scene on lid and engine-turned sides. Made in London in 1822. James Walker Collection.

31. Two of the miniature silver snuff boxes produced in Birmingham and London in considerable numbers in the 19th century. Left: A box made by Joseph Taylor in 1813. Right: Miniature oval box with engraved decoration made by Phipps and Robinson in 1800. James Walker Collection.

32. Typical castle top snuff box made by Nathaniel Mills in 1827. The subject of this box is Newstead Abbey. James Walker Collection.

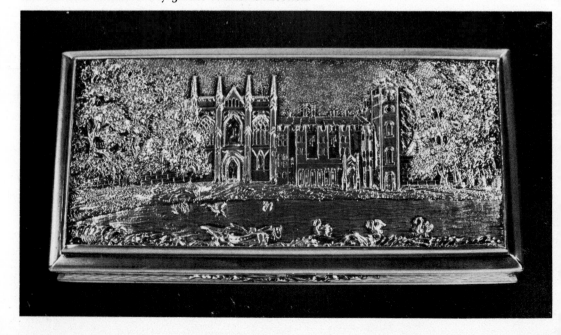

diamond-encrusted boxes which Frederick acquired for his collection or gave to visiting diplomats, leaves one in no doubt of the important rôle which this designer played in the development of what we now think of as the typical Frederick the Great snuff box.

When Frederick the Great invaded Silesia in 1741 much to the discomfiture of the young Maria-Theresa, he acquired the Silesian mines and so obtained access to an abundance of lovely apple-green chrysoprase, and to the other chalcedonies which these mines produced in profusion. It was from this pastel-green material that the bodies of the most memorable of the so-called Potsdam boxes, which were produced in Berlin exclusively for the King, were carved and then decorated in the Krüger manner. Similar boxes were also made from blue-black chalcedony and from a composition stained to the colour of turquoise, but it is those made from the translucent green material that were the most effective. These large table boxes were of baroque shape with deep bodies, and round the edges of the lids diamonds were set *en masse*, with tinted foils beneath some of the stones to give them colour. Diamonds of different sizes were set side by side to produce an encrustation with a swirling outline, obviously deriving from the rococo scrollwork with which Krüger must have become familiar in London and later in Paris. Within this lavish rococo frame, around the walls of the box and even on the base, asymmetric decoration was applied, also reminiscent in its composition of rococo repoussé chasing. The decoration on the Berlin boxes was, however, composed of gold inlaid in grooves in the chrysoprase. A golden pavilion among trees might be inlaid in a lid and then *pavé*-set with diamonds. A flower spray may consist of a bouquet of important diamonds set into inlays, and around this would be added flowers and leaves carved from coloured gem materials. They are still carved in this manner today in Idar Oberstein by glyptic artists working with small carborundum wheels and tiny drills like those used by dentists.

If these boxes of incredible splendour were reserved for the King and for those whom the King wished to flatter or cajole, and if indeed all gold boxes were the prerogative of the favoured few in Germany, there were still many types of snuff boxes which people of lesser pretensions could acquire. As has been mentioned elsewhere, there was in Germany a flourishing industry producing painted and printed enamelled copper boxes, imitating the more expensive porcelain boxes of Meissen. In the first half of the century, most of these came from the Berlin factory run by the Fromerys, father and son, in collaboration with C. F. Herold, the famous Meissen porcelain painter. The decoration on these boxes included conventional flower subjects, chinoiseries and allegories. Later during the Seven Years War the enamel painters produced propaganda boxes, and inside the lids or on the bases of some boxes are badly drawn erotica which might have served for illustrations for John Cleland's *Fanny Hill*.

Japanned papier-mâché boxes were also produced in Germany. Georg Siegmund Stobwasser was the best of the German makers for these. He settled in Brunswick in 1769 and produced large circular boxes lacquered black and decorated with reproductions of paintings of the period. The boxes usually bore the Stobwasser name, later combined with those who carried on his business after his death in 1776 until the middle years of the nineteenth century.

Undoubtedly the most famous of the boxes produced in non-precious materials in the Germany of the eighteenth century came from the Meissen porcelain factory at Dresden. The development of a European porcelain industry at the beginning of the eighteenth century came about as a result of trade with the East. Apart from bringing in tea and other exotic commodities from China and Japan, the merchants imported porcelain wares which were greatly admired. About 1706 in Dresden, a physicist, Ehrenfried Walther von Tschirnhausen, together with Johann Friedrich Böttger, an alchemist by trade, began to experiment to produce a hard paste like that used by the Chinese potters. Eventually they produced a mixture of an infusible china clay and feldspar, and a feldspar glaze that fused in the firing with the body to which it was applied, and by 1725 further refinements made it possible to produce a brilliant white porcelain similar to that made by the Chinese potters. In 1710 a factory was founded at Meissen, twelve miles from Dresden, which Böttger directed until his death in 1719. In 1720 a colour chemist and enamel painter from Berlin, Johann Gregor Herold, took over. He applied himself to devising a range of enamel colours which could be used to decorate the pottery. This decoration was applied over the glaze, and was either done in the factory or by outworkers known as *Hausmaler*. These painters worked from pattern books or from engravings of popular paintings, the work of the French artists such as Watteau and Boucher being very much in vogue in Germany during the second quarter of the century. Alternatively the art director of the factory, in this case, Herold, might create designs and hand them to the painters to copy, or even paint some pottery himself (see plate 25).

Some snuff boxes may have been produced in the early days at Meissen, but their production in quantity dates from 1735. This probably resulted from the interest of Count Heinrich von Brühl who became the director of the factory in 1733, and who in his lifetime collected no fewer than seven hundred gold snuff boxes. The Meissen boxes were of baroque form with deep bodies, which allowed paintings to be applied to the sides as well as to the top and to the inside of the lid. To the edge of the body and of the lid metal mounts were applied, usually of gold or silver, and the hinge was affixed to these. The subjects of the painting include renderings of French pictures, chinoiseries, landscapes and townscapes. Bonaventura Gottlieb Häuer, a painter who joined the Meissen factory in 1724, was responsible for a series of boxes depicting mining in Saxony, and other artists who may have been responsible for decorating surviving snuff boxes are J. G. Heintze who specialised in harbour scenes and the flower painter, Johann Gottfried Klinger. The paintings are hardly ever signed, and the identification of the work of a particular artist is therefore rather speculative.

From about 1755 boxes of different shapes began to be produced at Meissen, deep oblong ones being the most common, but round ones and basket-shaped ones were also produced. Trefoil and heart-shaped boxes also survive from this time, and even cane handles were produced with compartments for snuff in them.

In 1756 the Seven Years War began, and soon afterwards Frederick the Great's army actually occupied the Meissen factory. The King had plans for moving it in its entirety to Berlin but this proved to be impracticable. He satisfied himself, therefore, with placing large orders for snuff boxes and with transferring some of the best artists and craftsmen from Meissen to his own capital. Meissen was never to fully recover its domination of the porcelain industry in general and the snuff box trade in particular, for Frederick henceforward encouraged the production of boxes in Berlin at the expense of Meissen.

Long before this, rival factories were springing up all over Germany. To have one's own porcelain factory was becoming essential to the dignity of a German Elector, prince or duke. A porcelain factory could also, these petty rulers discerned, make a useful contribution to their exchequers. The secret of porcelain production, the arcanum, as it was called, could not be kept a secret for very long. A worker from Meissen turned up in Vienna with the formulae for the paste and the glaze, and the equally necessary knowledge of how to construct and operate a high-temperature kiln. This defection led to the founding of Claud du Paquier's Vienna factory that was subsequently to turn out snuff boxes, though not in any great quantity.

From Vienna the secret was carried to other areas. New porcelain factories were founded and existing faience factories became porcelain factories. By the middle of the century the Nymphenburg factory at Neudeck, established by the Elector of Bavaria in 1753, was offering snuff boxes painted with flowers or with landscapes at 5 florins each. Also in the snuff box business was the factory in the Landgrave of Hesse-Darmstadt at Kelsterbach, started in 1761, and the Duke Carl Eugen of Württemberg's factory at Ludwigsburg near Stuttgart where the production of porcelain began in 1758.

All these German porcelain factories marked the majority of their production. Meissen's famous blue crossed swords mark is to be found on most of the boxes from this factory (A-B below). This mark has been faked, and other factories have also used very similar marks, notably the Weesp factory in Holland from 1764 onwards, and later in the eighteenth century Worcester and the La Courtille factory in Paris used a crossed swords mark (C). The Volkstedt factory used similar looking crossed pitchforks from 1760 to 1787 (D). Fortunately, few if any of the factories employing pseudo-Meissen marks seem to have produced snuff boxes, certainly not in any great numbers.

One finds on Viennese porcelain snuff boxes a mark in the form of a shield from the Austrian arms. Berlin used a capital W, that just conceivably might be mistaken for the Meissen mark. Nymphenburg used an impressed hatched shield from the arms of Bavaria and, after 1765, sometimes a curious hexagram in blue (E-F). Kelsterbach used the monogram HD under a crown in blue and Ludwigsburg used crossed Cs under a crown and later, at the end of the century, three antlers from the Württemberg arms.

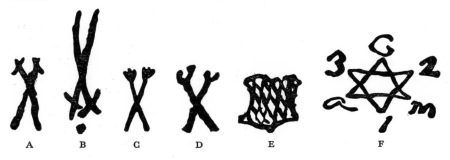

A   B   C   D   E   F

CHAPTER EIGHT

THE BEJEWELLED BOXES OF RUSSIA

When Peter the Great returned from England to his new city on the Neva delta in 1678, he was accompanied by some English gold workers. These were the first of hundreds of foreign gold-smiths who would be attracted in the course of the next century to the Court of St Petersburg. They would come from Germany, Sweden and Denmark, France and from England and Switzerland as well. Among these emigrant goldsmiths were the boxmakers who were to produce the fantastically rich Imperial boxes that can be seen today in the Gold Room in the Hermitage. To see these, wrote Kenneth Snowman

> is an experience which will always remain vivid in the memory. The nucleus of this breathtaking and extremely individual collection is the series of richly jewelled boxes which, in themselves, trace the dramatic, ruthless and often pathetic history of the rulers of this vast land.[1]

The earliest box in this collection of Imperial snuff boxes is an interesting memento box, a relatively unostentatious one, which was Peter the Great's favourite snuff box. It is in the form of the hull of a three-masted Dutch ship, carved from walnut and with a golden figurehead in the form of a lion. It would have recalled for its owner the time when he worked as a shipwright in the Amsterdam shipyards, lived a life of great simplicity and was apparently very happy. The box may have been made for him in Holland, or it may have been carved in Russia after Peter's return to his native country.

Much more in the Russian Imperial taste were the royal boxes made between 1715 and 1740, bearing royal cyphers set with diamonds and surrounded by diamond-set motifs. Though those who made the Russian boxes were foreign craftsmen whose work

[1] Snowman, *op. cit.*

118

reflected German and French taste, they catered to their new royal patrons by loading the decoration on lids and sides with diamonds.

The pleasure-loving Russian Empresses were great patrons of the foreign boxmakers. The Empress Elizabeth rewarded her lovers and friends with gifts of expensive boxes, and Catherine the Great carried on the tradition. Among those who provided these lavish boxes were makers of great technical ability and considerable taste. One of these was the Swiss Jérémie Pauzié. He was born in Geneva in 1716, and as a boy of thirteen travelled with his father to Hamburg where he embarked for St Petersburg. Once there he was apprenticed to a French goldsmith called Gravero. Pauzié became his own master in 1740, and was later appointed a court goldsmith by Catherine the Great. Pauzié did not sign his boxes, but a number of boxes which show the influence of the French artist Meissonnier, who was among those who introduced the rococo style, are generally attributed to him. Pauzié's boxes differ from the French rococo boxes in that the vigorous asymmetric scrolls are decked out with diamonds, a hundred or more sizable stones being set in a lid measuring no more than 7·5 cm. × 6·5 cm.

In 1770 a French boxmaker, Jean-Pierre Ador, arrived in St Petersburg from Paris. He and Johann Gottlieb Scharff, a goldsmith of German parentage who was born in Moscow and who had set up a workshop in St Petersburg in 1772, produced the finest of all the Imperial boxes. Their work can be identified with certainty, because from 1741 it became obligatory for a maker to add his mark to the town mark of St Petersburg—a double-headed eagle from 1730 to 1742, and from 1742 to 1825 crossed anchors and a sceptre with the date below.

Many of Ador's boxes are in the French style. The famous deep oblong box by him in the Smithsonian Institute in Washington, recording Catherine the Great's *coup d'état* on June 27, 1762, is similar to the boxes featuring the gouache paintings of Van Blarenberghe, though inevitably Ador gave the Russian paintings a diamond-set frame. There is also an elegant large oblong box in the Hermitage attributed to him, decorated with reverse painting in enamel that might have been made in Paris. This box is peculiar in that the decorative panels are reversible, being

119

decorated on the reverse with a diaper pattern. Bands of blue *basse-taille* enamel enclose golden diamond-shaped areas engraved with sunbursts. An oval box of his in the Louvre has Susannah and the Elders painted *en plein* on the lid together with chased gold classical architectural motifs, which again might be a French box though the enamel painting is not as good as the best French work. A number of oval boxes, produced by Ador about 1775, show that he had learnt by then to cater to Russian taste for opulence, using diamonds as lavishly as the other foreign box-makers who had found royal favour in St Petersburg.

Perhaps because of his German ancestry and because he was trained by a German called Goebelt, Scharff seems from the outset to have been in sympathy with the rich effects demanded by the Russian court. He was an outstanding technician and a fine artist and produced boxes which were at once rich, pretty and urbane. His boxes were not just a form of portable wealth of no great inspiration as were those of many of his contemporaries. The round and oval boxes made by him in 1776 and 1777 are the finest examples of the boxmaker's art in the Hermitage collection, though their intrinsic value was slight compared with the work of less talented makers which surrounds them. One of these boxes, only 6·5 cms in diameter, is enamelled white and on the lid are six delicate circlets of stones, rubies and diamonds. In the centre is a tiny enamel plaque after Lancret. Another of these boxes has a little plaque on the lid depicting Catherine the Great's favourite greyhound, and round this is a delicate and imaginative diamond-and-emerald-set trellis above an opaque brown enamel ground.

Snuff-taking was very much of a courtly habit in eighteenth-century Russia, and it was not until about 1780 that the demand for modest boxes by the less affluent led to the emergence of a silver box industry. Over the next seventy years these silver boxes became familiar throughout Europe. The early boxes were usually circular like the gold boxes of the period, but the later ones are rectangular. These boxes were almost always decorated with niello. This technique of decoration resembles champlevé enamelling, but a compound of lead, silver and copper mixed with borax and sulphur is heaped in powder form into the engraved channels cut into the silver surface. Then the box is stoved, producing a black linear design contrasting with the surrounding silver. The decoration used was enormously varied. Some boxes were decorated with landscapes, others with pastoral scenes. There were also memento boxes on which famous monuments or maps were depicted, while city plans seem also to have been popular with the buying public in Russia.

CHAPTER NINE

EIGHTEENTH-CENTURY DUTCH BOXES

The Dutch were a nation of pipe smokers, and relatively few Dutch men or women took snuff at any period. As a result Dutch snuff boxes are very rare indeed, but the few that do exist are very interesting and some of them are very fine.

It is probable that a handful of people living in the Netherlands were taking snuff as early as the seventeenth century, but few of the accoutrements of snuff-taking survive in Holland that can be definitely ascribed to this period and which are undoubtedly of Dutch origin. There are, in the Neimeyer collection in Amsterdam, a number of ivory snuff rasps that could date from the late seventeenth century, but it is by no means certain that they were made in Holland. They are very similar to those French rasps that belonged to the late Edward Pinto which are now in the Birming-ham Museum and Art Gallery, and one suspects that they could well be French. Of course, they may have been made by French ivory workers, who like the Obrissets were Huguenots, and who escaped persecution in Amsterdam. Questionable also are two tortoise-shell boxes decorated with *piqué posé* work, which are in the Neimeyer museum. They, too, could be late seventeenth-century productions, but may not be Dutch. For good reasons museum curators and authors often fall back on the safe description, "English or Continental", when faced with these tortoise-shell piqué boxes.

It is only when one comes to look at the gold and silver boxes of the eighteenth century in the Rijksmuseum and in the Dutch private collections, that one finds oneself on firmer ground. Many of these bear marks which, thanks very largely to the research of Karel Citroen, can be attributed. These boxes are mostly the works of expatriate Huguenot goldsmiths from Paris and Blois, who towards the close of the seventeenth century settled in two little streets off the Kalverstraat in Amsterdam, the Handboogstraat and Voetboogstraat. These French émigrés supported themselves in the first instance, it is believed, by making cases for the Dutch watchmakers, and it is interesting in this connection that one of the earliest extant Dutch snuff boxes, now in the Rijksmuseum collection, is nothing more nor less than a repoussé silver watch case with a lid hinged to it. This little box, which was made about 1667, is illustrated on plate 26. It reminds us that the Dutch are often given the credit for inspiring the English watch case and snuff box makers to decorate their work with religious and allegorical scenes in repoussé.

The most accomplished gold boxes produced in Holland in the eighteenth century were the work of a Huguenot maker of whom nothing is known beyond the fact that he worked in Amsterdam and had the initials I.S. The best known of I.S.'s boxes is the one with an architectural motif on the lid in the Rijksmuseum, illustrated in plate 27. It was made at a time (1739) when for once in her history Holland was an extremely prosperous country and her merchants could well afford luxuries. It is as fine as any of the French repoussé boxes of the period. So too is the Jacques Girardin box from a Dutch private collection, illustrated in plate 22.

One early eighteenth-century Dutch repoussé box does exist that does not look like the urbane work of a French chaser, but has a strong Dutch accent. This is the so-called De Peyster box in the New York Historical Society Collection. This silver box made about 1720 has the De Peyster arms on the lid, crowned by a surround of repoussé figures. More interesting is the base of the box, which has a nubile-looking Susannah flanked by two lecherous elders. The Dutch artists had a great penchant for this parable, not so much, in the opinion of Karel Citroen, because of its religious context, but because it provided in this strait-laced country an acceptable opportunity to depict a naked woman.

Some of the later Dutch gold snuff boxes may also have been made and decorated by Dutchmen. There is one in the Wartski collection made by a Louis Mestejer whose name suggests that he was probably a Dutchman, but it is very much in the Huguenot style. One wonders if Mestejer was perhaps apprenticed to one of the Huguenots.

Dutch eighteenth-century silver boxes are even rarer than gold ones. There are a few in the Rijksmuseum, and the one with an engraved horse-drawn sleigh on the lid, made in 1727 in Middelburg (plate 28) is almost certainly one of those great rarities, a Dutch snuff box unquestionably made by a Dutch craftsman. A plain box, of similar baroque form, made in Northern Holland in the 1720s is another.

Holland is no happy hunting ground for the snuff box collector. Even nineteenth-century Dutch boxes are rare, and those that do exist are for the most part copies of the silver boxes that were made in the factories of Sheffield and Birmingham. Nonetheless, such eighteenth-century Dutch snuff boxes as do exist are interesting because they illustrate the effects of the Revocation of the Edict of Nantes in exporting French culture to the protestant countries of Europe. They show too how the influx of French craftsmen continued to influence culture, metropolitan culture at least, in these countries for over half a century.

CHAPTER TEN

EUROPEAN INFLUENCES IN AMERICA

Quite a number of silver boxes were made in the United States of America from the 1720s onwards. But how many of these are in fact snuff boxes is an open question. A box made by John Coney of Boston, the first recorded American boxmaker, is in the Yale University Art Gallery. The Coney box is a typical example of American work with its loose lid. It is of the flat oval type, similar to those early eighteenth-century English boxes which are usually designated tobacco boxes. Coney was obviously a competent craftsman. This box is well made, and the intricately engraved coat of arms on the lid, probably that of the Lieutenant-Governor of New Hampshire, John Wentworth, is well drawn. It seems hardly conceivable that a boxmaker of Coney's ability could have been unaware of the practical advantages of a hinged lid on a portable snuff box, and was perfectly capable of making a hinge had he wished to do so. The probable reasons why this and the majority of the other early American boxes were made with loose lids was because they were intended for smoking tobacco. Conceivably, however, they could have been intended as table snuff boxes for use in home or tavern.

A very few hinged boxes made in the 1720s do survive. There are two in the Henry Ford Museum at Dearborne in Michigan, for example, both of which were owned by women, and these are almost certainly snuff boxes. One of these, with the name of its owner Catharina De Peyster engraved on the base, has a heavily repousséd lid depicting a plump cherub. So unusual is repoussé chasing in America at this date that one cannot help wonder if the lid, like its owner, was not native-born American but of Dutch origin. One inevitably calls to mind that other repoussé box mentioned in Chapter Nine which was also owned by a De Peyster. The other American box, which is inscribed "Ann Parcivell Her Box 1729", is a plain oval box with a flat-hinged lid.

The owner's name was also often engraved on those loose-lidded boxes which were far more common than the hinged ones. These boxes had a naïve charm. Many of them are oval, though heart-shaped ones do exist. Most of the surviving examples were probably made in the 1740s, though it must be appreciated that the dating of all these American boxes is problematical as the only marks on them are maker's marks, and some of them do not even have these. The only type of decoration on these boxes is engraving, usually very unsophisticated, like the quatrefoil of a child-like simplicity on a box which William Huertin Jr made about 1740. A decorative motif found on many of these boxes was a border of what would seem to be intended to be either oak leaves or husks (plate 29). This border was a characteristic feature of Albany boxes, but is also found on boxes made in other places.

Snuff-taking was not a popular habit in America before the middle of the century, and was mainly restricted to European officials and wealthy merchants. One cannot believe that the naïve native boxes would have been much to the taste of the establishment. Those people who brought the snuffing habit from Europe probably also brought their boxes with them, or later imported them from England, Holland or France. Even as late as 1759 there was apparently a demand for imported boxes. In that year the Philadelphia silversmith, John Leacock, placed an announcement in the *Pennsylvania Gazette* to the effect that he had imported from London "chased snuff boxes, gilt the inside". Some local makers were, however, by this time beginning to vie with the European makers by producing more stylish boxes. A box in the Philadelphia Museum of Art shows that in 1757 Joseph Richardson, another Philadelphia silversmith, was certainly catering for the more fashion-conscious American snuff-taker. This baroque form box has a repoussé-chased rococo lid that is very sophisticated by American standards of the time. It is interesting in this context too, that an emigré London maker, Daniel Fueter, advertised in a New York paper in 1763 that he had acquired the services of a Mr John Anthony Beau, a "chaiser from Geneva".

In the 1750s and 1760s silver-mounted shell boxes like those popular in Europe were made in considerable numbers in America and the chasing on the lids of these is very competently carried out. John Leacock produced a particularly fine one about 1759, as good as anything he could have imported from Europe. About 1770 yet another Philadelphia maker, Daniel Dupuy, whose name suggests he may have been of French origin, was producing those deep oval boxes with a central motif on the lid in the Louis Seize style.

American snuff boxes are like all provincial work, for the most part inferior copies of the products of the leading makers of the day, but there are the oddities among provincial pieces which delight us, and these boxes often have a charm which results from the imperfect technique of their makers.

PART THREE

CHAPTER ONE

ENGLISH BOXES IN THE 1800s

By the middle of the nineteenth century snuffing would no longer be a fashionable habit, but when the century began there was no sign that in only a few decades snuff-taking would have been replaced in polite society by the puffing of cigars and pipes, and by the new fad of cigarette smoking. In the early 1800s snuffing was as popular as ever, and as the cartoons of the period reveal it was practised by all strata of society. These cartoons depict the young bucks in the clubs of St James's dipping in their snuff boxes; one of Gillray's obese squires flourishing his box; a half tipsy, half blind, old crone in a torn dress finding solace in snuff; Scotsmen in kilts and a sailor with a peg leg are caught in the act of snuff-taking, and as a last favour, a condemned man on the gallows is given a parting pinch.

Amongst the aristocracy the habit flourished as never before. As has already been indicated, the ledgers of Fribourg and Treyer read like pages from Debrett, with the King and his family heading the list of illustrious customers. The King bought snuff, specially blended for him by the firm, by the pound. Others, too, had their tastes for exotic snuffs specially catered for by the firm, whose ledgers list, for example, the Duke of Rutland's sort and Lord Edward Bentinck's sort. Fribourg and Treyer supplied the regimental messes of the day too, and of course they were not the only snuff house favoured by influential customers. There were Wishart and Company at the sign of the Highlander, Thistle and Crown in Coventry Street, the founder of the business having been a supporter of the Young Pretender's cause, and there was John Hardhan in Fleet Street and Pontet in Pall Mall among them.

Perhaps the most avid snuff-taker of all time was a customer of Fribourg and Treyer. This was Lord Petersham, later the Earl of Harrington, who in 1819 showed his appreciation of the firm's services by presenting George Evans, who directed the Haymarket shop at this time, with an inscribed gold-lined amboyna snuff box.[1] Sacheverell Sitwell relates that "one room of Harrington House, the old family mansion off Whitehall, was filled with shelves bearing Chinese jars of great beauty which held the various kinds of snuff". Lord Petersham was equally addicted to tea and the room also contained jars of this, and, "this sacred room was presided over by an eccentric individual who blended the teas and prepared the snuffs for their noble owner". In fact this was "a sort of dispensary of tea and snuff, a private emporium into which it would be a delight to enter".[2]

While such houses as Fribourg and Treyer blended snuffs to suit the cultivated tastes of the King and the nobility, the demand obviously also continued for beautiful boxes to contain these exotic powders. In cramped workshops, men of great skill, acquired during long apprenticeships, laboured over bench and hearth to fashion and decorate gold into gracious and fashionable confections for the snuffers of the new century. Lord Petersham collected boxes as he collected snuff. Like all the great collectors before him he was said to have "used a different box on every day of the year". And he was not alone in his avidity for golden boxes.

Excellent, in terms of craftsmanship, as many of these nineteenth-century gold snuff boxes were, something of the delicacy, the inventiveness, the inspiration had gone. In France the old rigid standards had been swept away when the revolution disbanded the old Guild of Goldsmiths, but the artistic deterioration was not alone the result of the political expediency, which destroyed a body which had demonstrated over the course of a century that gold box making could be raised to the level of an art form. Nor could the Industrial Revolution take all the blame in England. At one time it was usual to suggest that the Industrial Revolution was at the root of a certain lack of taste which pervades much of the applied art of the early nineteenth century. But was it probably not just that the new century inherited tired traditions and ideas and evolved, at the outset at least, few new ones of its own? One detects that the goldsmiths were, in the early years of the century, repeating by rote the time-honoured forms and motifs of another age, without conviction or understanding.

[1] Evans, *op. cit.*
[2] Sitwell, *op. cit.*

It is not without significance perhaps that the most satisfying of the early nineteenth-century boxes were those produced in the Birmingham factories for the middle-class snuffers of the day. While these Midland boxmakers might sometimes pay lip service to neo-classicism, generally speaking they evolved their own styles—their own shapes and decorative motifs. They chased, or engraved or engine-turned the silver surfaces of their boxes to produce simple patterns of dots or diapers, repeated patterns of barley or fox head, sometimes adding a central garland, or an arabesque or one of those floral sprays which were to be the predominant motif of the century. It was subtle decoration, a dainty embellishment of a beautiful, unpretentious metal.

These boxes did not miraculously appear in 1800, a new style born for a new century. Throughout the eighteenth century silver boxes had been produced in Birmingham, and for a decade or more before the nineteenth century began men like Samuel Pemberton had been producing boxes which one would be inclined to classify as early nineteenth-century in manner. The bright-cut decoration, however, declare them to be earlier. Such a box by the Birmingham makers, Willmore and Alston, was included in the exhibition celebrating the bicentenary of the Birmingham Assay Office in 1973. There was another by Pemberton himself in this same exhibition. Nor had silver box making in this style been confined to Birmingham. Nobody produced finer examples than Phipps and Robinson in London. Eric Delieb illustrates a fine box[1] which this partnership produced as early as 1787, an oval double box, bright-cut all over with a leaf and diaper pattern, and with richly bright-cut walls. The foundations of the new style were already laid. When the new century opened, wealth spread into new hands and Victorian morality decreed that ostentation must be avoided at all costs. This led to the mass-production of these simple silver boxes. In the first fifty years of the nineteenth century restrained, workmanlike silver snuff boxes were produced in their thousands in Birmingham and London.

Though the makers of these silver boxes—men like Joseph Taylor, the Linwoods and the Mills and Pemberton—were induced to repeat successful patterns, there is no lack of variety

[1] Delieb, Eric, *Silver Boxes,* Herbert Jenkins, 1968.

to maintain the interest of the collector of these fascinating items. If there is such a thing as the classical box of the period, it is the oblong box with rounded corners, round the edges of which bold, chased-up fancy wires were soldered on so that they stood proud of lid and base. Within this frame the lid was usually barley engine-turned all over, except for a plain oval or cartouche-shaped area in the centre designed to take the owner's initials. Sometimes, particularly on gold and gilded examples, the decoration is more elaborate, consisting of repoussé-chased work, or more usually at this period, chased-up cast relief panels.

Sometimes the imagery of the previous century was rehashed for the repoussé panels of early nineteenth-century boxes. There is, for instance, a box now in the property of the Birmingham assay office, made by Linwood in 1816. It is decorated with rococo allegorical decoration, with scrolls, fruit, leaves and a goddess all depicted with that lifelessness that is a feature of so much nineteenth-century revivalism produced by provincial craftsmen. When, however, these same craftsmen turned to the contemporary scene for inspiration their work had much more conviction. There is in the James Walker collection (plate 30) a deep oblong table box made in 1822 by William Eaton which illustrates this. It depicts, in high relief repoussé chasing, hounds following a fox over a brushwood fence, and the rendering is extremely lively. A box of similar form, produced by that fine London maker, John Linnett, in 1824, has an all-over chased pattern of flowers and scrolls. This box, which the inscription in the central rococo cartouche tells us was a gift from the Laird of Drumcrosshall to the Laird of Stratton, is an example of nineteenth-century craftsmanship at its best, the chaser employing characteristic Victorian motifs to produce a box of great charm. The Victorian craftsmen were seldom as successful in depicting the human figure as they were when they turned to landscapes and floral motifs, but now and again they did depict genre scenes which had a naïve charm. Such a box was made by Gervase Wheeler of Birmingham in 1838. This has a relief plaque applied to the engine-turned lid, and this relief plaque depicts a violinist accompanied by a woman on the piano, the scene enclosed within a rather clumsy rococo-scrolled frame.

Another popular type of box in the nineteenth century was an oval box with rounded corners which was bowed, presumably so that it fitted more comfortably in a pocket. Samuel Pemberton produced a very charming box in this form in 1809 with a lattice pattern which has two compartments in it. The shallow compartment under the lid lifts on a hinge to reveal the second compartment. If it was designed, as it presumably was, to contain two different sorts of snuff, it must have been quite a feat on the part of its owner to get at the lower container without spilling the contents of the upper one. Another box of this kind, made in Birmingham by Thomas Tompson in 1808, was among those shown at the Birmingham Museum and Art Gallery in the bicentenary exhibition of 1973.

Perhaps, however, the most delightful of all the charming silver boxes produced in Birmingham and London in the course of this century were the miniatures. These boxes, possibly made for women snuffers, were 2·5 cm. or less in length. Both Joseph Taylor and Samuel Pemberton, among others, produced boxes of this type. Two typical examples are illustrated in plate 31. The box made by Joseph Taylor in 1813 with a floral cartouche between chequerwork is 2·5 cm. long and weighs only 0·15 ounces. The oval box was made by Phipps and Robinson, with an all-over chequer pattern and is slightly more substantial, weighing 0·24 ounces. The Taylor box is hinged, as most of these little boxes are, but the other box has a loose lid.

Another interesting type of Birmingham box was the "castle-top". These boxes were decorated, as the name implies, with repoussé representations of some of Britain's famous castles. This form of decoration is more common on vignettes than on snuff boxes, but quite a number of the latter were produced, featuring the massive towers of Windsor or the gothic intricacies of Newstead Abbey (plate 32). Another favourite subject of these boxes, which were produced by Nathaniel Mills, Taylor and Perry, Joseph Willmore and Edward Smith, was one featuring Abbotsford, Sir Walter Scott's home. The boxmakers sometimes represented cathedrals or palaces or town halls, or other public buildings on their lids. Again, sometimes instead of being carried out repoussé within a bold decorative wire border, the representations of the buildings were chased or engraved on a flat lid. In the 1850s, for example, the Crystal Palace was a popular motif and this was invariably engraved. Castle-tops are incidentally still being produced in pewter by James Dixon of Sheffield.

Though the Birmingham boxmakers of the nineteenth century are rightly famous, their work often has a provincial flavour about it when compared with the work of the leading London makers. To compare the engraving on the box by Rawlings and Summers shown in plate 33 with typical Birmingham work of the period, is to appreciate that provincial competence was one thing, metropolitan sophistication quite another. And even if one accepts that this London box is an unusually fine example of the engraver's art, it nevertheless illustrates what London could, and frequently did, produce. John Linnett's boxes, too, were almost always very beautifully chased, including those curious repoussé boxes from his workshop depicting a spirit pedlar in early eighteenth-century costume, which was one of his specialities. One of these was, incidentally, sold at Christie's in 1969 and fetched no less than 620 guineas.

Another of the oddities of this period were the form boxes in the shape of a fox's mask. Nathaniel Mills produced these, and one by this maker, hallmarked in 1830, appeared in the Birmingham bicentenary exhibition, having been loaned by the Birmingham Assay Office. Very similar in conception are the pair of tiny silver gilt eagle head boxes in the James Walker collection (plate 34). Silver-mounted cowrie shell boxes continued to be made too. Delieb illustrates one, by London maker G. Read, produced as late as 1883. Gone from the lid of this box, however, is the flowing decoration that characterised those of the previous century. In its place there is a formality verging on monotony, resulting from the decoration of the whole expanse of the lid with an engine-turned pattern. This is done more than competently. The circles of ropework are reduced in width as they are reduced in size towards the centre, and the whole is a *tour de force* of the engine-turned art, but it does not accord with the cowrie shell below it. It is all too mechanical. If one looks at the gracious lid of the eighteenth-century cowrie shell box in plate 35, one feels that here summed up in two pieces are the essential differences between the silversmithing of the two centuries. To suggest that the one is the product of an artist craftsman while the other is the product of the factory, is to project a too romantic view of the eighteenth-century scene, but one is certainly in the craft tradition, while the other belongs to the age of the machine—to an age that set too much store by accuracy. It was against such lack of soul that William Morris was to lead his revolt. As we have seen, the nineteenth century produced many charming silver boxes and many elegant ones too, but they are, compared with eighteenth-century boxes, often a little lifeless, a little laboured.

The London and Birmingham makers turned out some large table boxes, some so very large that they must have been intended for the convivial gatherings of clubs. Most of these were rather ponderous boxes, often repoussé-chased on the lid, and lacking the charms of the smaller pocket boxes.

The silver ones were by no means the only snuff boxes produced in England during the nineteenth century. Gold boxes, as has already been indicated, continued to be made. To begin with, these were usually in the old Louis Seize style, for fashions do not promptly lose their following with the turn of the century. There is an oval snuff box, for example, in the Royal Scottish Museum in Edinburgh, hallmarked in London in 1808/9 with a portrait of a lady between engine-turned panels covered with transparent enamel, which might have been made at any time during the previous thirty years by a rather uninspired craftsman.

By the end of the second decade of the century gold boxes began to be made in styles popularised by the London and Birmingham makers of silver boxes, and these are much more interesting than the earlier pastiches. Some of these shallow oblong boxes had no more than simple ribbed decoration, but the most popular design was the curved-cornered box with a raised wire edge. Others, like one sold at Christie's in 1972 and made by A. J. Strachan in London in 1818, were more complex in conception. This box has a border of multi-coloured golds chased to represent the rose, the thistle and the shamrock—symbols of England, Scotland and Ireland—the centre of the lid being the usual engine-turned panel. A more typical gold box from this period, however, was that shown by Wartski at the 1973 Antique Dealers Fair in London, a box made by John Northam in 1819. This has incurving sides and is all over engine-turned; the thumbpiece is a mass of floral chasing (plate 36). Such simple box designs look elegant in gold and handle nicely, the weight of the gold giving them an important feel. They are also invariably beautifully made. Less happy are the repoussé gold boxes of the period like that in the Antique Porcelain Company collection in New York, which was made in London in 1815. The repoussé hunting scene is lively and well drawn, but the designer has provided it with a ponderous frame of gold acanthus leaves that gives the box a nineteenth-century pomposity.

Aside from the gold and silver boxes the nineteenth-century English manufacturers catered for every taste and every pocket with boxes made from every conceivable material. They used lava from Mount Vesuvius, the blue massive fluorspar from Castleton in Derbyshire and painted slate from the same county. Boxes were made from Sheffield plate in Birmingham, wooden boxes were made in great variety (Fribourg and Treyer charged from 7 shillings to two guineas each for them). Tortoise-shell boxes remained popular, but were expensive, and papier-mâché boxes were readily available to the snuffer of modest means. Thomas Hubball of Clerkenwell invented his "bronzes", metallic powders which were used to add brightness, and subtler decoration to these japanned papier-mâché boxes, although painted decoration remained the most popular form of embellishment. George Evans, in his history of Fribourg and Treyer, stated that the lids of these boxes were decorated with "paintings . . . the subjects generally being landscapes, figures and scenes in life, the latter being often of a rather coarse nature". Evans also drew attention to the use of vegetable matter in the making of these boxes as a substitute for paper, and illustrates a "potato box" made from potato skins. "These potato boxes", he wrote,

> were ornamented with a lacquer of greenish shade, with a few fine streaks of red or gold. They were frequently ornamented with a crest, monogram, or some neat design in gold on the lid. The hinges were metal, and generally a little clumsy. Twelve shillings was about the price of these, though at this price there would be little or no gold ornamentation."[1]

Evans also mentioned boxes made from other vegetable matter which were listed in the firm's books but admitted that he had never seen one of these.

[1] Evans, *op. cit.*

It was at this period that the Prescot watchmakers, hard hit by French competition, turned their skill to making brass snuff boxes. These Lancashire brass snuff boxes are interesting if not beautiful. Many of them were of watch case form, but shuttle-shaped boxes decorated with bright-cutting were also made. The most interesting of these boxes are those to which their makers applied their knowledge of miniature mechanisms, supplying them with combination locks. These were opened by dialling a code on a pair of watch hands pivoted in the centres of engraved chapter rings on the lid.

CHAPTER TWO

SWISS ENAMELLED BOXES

The art of enamel painting had been revived in Geneva in the 1780s. In the seventeenth century the Geneva enamellers had been famous, their decorated watch cases being in demand all over Europe. But the craft had died out towards the end of the century, partly perhaps because of a change of fashion but mainly, one suspects, because these enamel paintings had proved to deteriorate in use. With the revival of interest in enamel decoration in the second half of the eigtheenth century and the evolution of a transparent coating which would protect painted enamels, the craft was revived in Geneva and prospered there for over a century. Though this revival began in the eighteenth century—there were already 77 enamellers working in the city by 1789—the majority of the surviving boxes dare from the nineteenth century.

The early Swiss snuff boxes, those produced by the Geneva enamellers in the later years of the eighteenth century, are similar to the Paris boxes from the same period. A typical example of Geneva work from the 1780s was the box sold at Christie's in 1973, shown in plate 37. It has the usual central medallion, depicting what appears to be a Roman soldier to whom a woman is presenting her child, the woman being dressed in eighteenth-century costume, the figures standing in a Watteauesque background. On either side of them edallion are the usual *guilloché* panels, scattered with stars and covered with transparent enamel. It was not until the nineteenth century that the Geneva enamellers evolved a recognisable style of their own.

The nineteenth-century Swiss enamelled snuff box was usually a shallow oblong one with canted or curved corners, though the Geneva smallworkers produced lobbed oval boxes and occasionally other fancy shapes too. The enamel paintings which were featured on the lids and sides and bases of these boxes, and which sometimes decorated the interiors as well, usually depicted the local landscapes though pastoral and allegorical paintings were also popular. The landscapes were highly romanticised, sometimes to the point of mawkishness, though technically highly accomplished. Kenneth Snowman, that great connoisseur and authority on gold boxes, is very scathing about these "extremely banal glimpses in enamel of local scenic splendour". He wrote:

> The artistic cliché in fact, saw its apotheosis on the banks of Lac Léman at this period. Occasionally no fewer than four of these lakescapes entirely cover both sides, inside and out, of the lid and floor of a fancy-shaped Swiss gold box—the cumulative effect of this repetition when the box is opened, far from increasing its precious quality, merely serves to remind one unmistakably of those stands or windmills of coloured postcards, eternal revolving guardians of the alpine scene . . . A justifiable criticism of the Swiss Box is that seeing one, in the mind's eye, one tends to see whole shelves of them; they have been formally ordered, efficiently executed and promptly delivered rather than pondered on, lovingly fashioned and proudly handed over to a new owner."[1]

One might add other criticisms of these boxes to those listed by Kenneth Snowman. The figure work, when it appears, is stiff and provincial, while the Geneva enamellers were inclined to elaborate excessively the surrounds to their pictures, as though carried away by their own technical virtuosity. This lack of restraint is well illustrated by the box pictured in plate 38. The landscape in the centre, which incidentally epitomises Geneva enamel painting, is almost overwhelmed by the supporting cornucopia filled with lifeless fruit, while the two shell motifs in the corners are totally irrelevant distractions. Faced with a box like this, one cannot feel that Snowman was being too harsh.

In fairness to the Geneva tradition, however, it must be said that not all the boxes produced there in the nineteenth century were this bad, artistically speaking. The other box illustrated in plate 38 has more to recommend it. The painting is the work of the most famous of the Geneva artists, Jean-Louis Richter. The paintings on this particular box are in fact signed "Jean-Louis Richter and Aimé Julien Troll" but what part Troll played in

[1] Snowman, *op. cit.*

141

the work is not known. Richter's painting, while typical of the Geneva work of the period in being soft and sentimental, has more strength and artistic merit than that of most of his contemporaries. This is indeed a rather pretty box. The lobbed oval shape is charming and must have made considerable demands on the goldsmith called upon to form it. The box itself came from the workshop of a goldsmith called A. Magnim and is, like most of the boxes on which the enamels were painted, an extremely competent piece of goldsmithing. The border decoration on this box is much more restrained, as is that on most of Richter's boxes. This formal floral border derives, of course, from Paris. Individually, Richter boxes are really very pleasing. Somehow, seen in isolation, the paintings have a period charm, but to visit the Museum of Art and History of Geneva and to see them in the mass, is to discover just how apt is the label "carte postale" which Snowman has applied to them.

Not all the Swiss boxes of this period featured landscape painting. Quite a number of floral boxes were produced, like the little lobbed oval boxes shown in plate 39. One of these has a floral and musical trophy on the lid, surrounded by a ribbon-wrapped floral wreath. This is a charming little box, but if one looks beyond the general effectiveness of the decoration one becomes aware that the painting is very stiff and the flowers are like the landscapes, too good to be real. It is curious that even the plainest of the Swiss boxes, those that are decorated only with engine-turning within an enamelled floral border, still somehow manage to appear overloaded and oversweet.

The Swiss genius lies perhaps more towards the mechanical than towards the arts. They produced automata during the nineteenth century of incredible complexity, and the presiding genius of automata making was Jaquet-Droz, whose works on the large scale are the chief attraction of the Neuchâtel Museum. Automata were applied to watches and to snuff boxes as well, little performances taking place on an inner lid as the musical boxes within ground out their trifling tunes.

A particularly rich octagonal box of this type, made in 1825, was sold by Christie's in 1963. This box had originally been given to Elena Pavlovna, wife of Grand Duke Michael of Russia, by her mother-in-law. Depicted on the lid is a musical party, with the owner's monogram set with diamonds on a blue enamel background over the performing figures. These automata boxes were innocent, diverting toys for an age that clamoured for novelties—almost always innocent, that is. The Swiss discovered that among their many customers for watches and enamelled snuff boxes in the Middle East were some with a penchant for pornography. Bo Bramsen illustrates an example, and a fairly typical one, of the results of this trade, an automata snuff box of 1810 on which are depicted two soldiers and two girls having intercourse.

The most famous of the Swiss automata boxes were of course the singing bird boxes. These usually have a little oval cover in the centre of the lid, which flips up to reveal the bird that then begins to pirouette, to flap its wings and to sing its brief song. There is some evidence to suggest that these boxes were originally a French invention, but it was the Swiss who exploited the idea. Again the most famous maker of these boxes was Jaquet-Droz, who exported them all over the world.

It is perhaps not surprising that the Swiss watchmakers and boxmakers sometimes joined forces, and one does find quite a number of Swiss boxes into which a watch has been built. These watches are seldom found in working condition, however, which is hardly to be wondered at, for, as was indicated in an earlier chapter, one would hardly conceive of anything more calculated to clog a watch mechanism than snuff.

Few Swiss boxes, either the Geneva ones or those made elsewhere in Switzerland, are marked other than with the initials or, occasionally, the signature of the maker. One does come across Swiss boxes made between 1801 and 1814 which bear French hallmarks, however, and it has been wrongly suggested that these marks were an attempt on the part of the Geneva makers to give their boxes the cachet of a Paris origin. Anyone who knows these people and their pride in all things Swiss would find this theory hard to credit, and there is a perfectly simple explanation, of course, for the presence of those French marks. During this period Geneva was under French rule, and wherever the French dominated they imposed their bureaucratic systems, including their government-controlled hallmarking system. One also finds French hallmarks on goldwares made in Italy and in the Low Countries, two other areas to come under French domination.

CHAPTER THREE

SCANDINAVIAN BOXES OF THE 1800s

In Scandinavia the ridiculous Captain Puff flourished his snuff box in the street, dignitaries at some no doubt important meeting greeted one another with outstretched snuff boxes; a gentleman with literary pretensions relieved the boredom of a poetry-reading with a pinch of snuff; in the fields a farm worker offered his wife a pinch from his box, and of an evening in the farm kitchen, as the company listened to the fiddle player seated on the floor, the snuff was passed round. There are no statistics of snuff-taking at this period, but the Swedish and Norwegian and Danish artists of the time leave us in no doubt that in the new century, as in the old one, people in all walks of life in Scandinavia enjoyed their snuff. And as the habit continued to flourish so the silver boxmakers of Copenhagen, Stockholm and Bergen continued to thrive.

The Scandinavian makers had always drawn most of their inspiration from Paris, and a Paris fashion having been adopted, it tended to linger longer in the north. It has been noted that the rococo style was still flourishing there as late as 1780, and, in the same way, the Louis Seize style still remained fashionable there long after it had disappeared from the Paris scene, even as late as 1846. It was not until about 1840 that the shallow rectangular box with rounded corners, a style already established in England three or four decades earlier, gained widespread popularity in Denmark, Norway and Sweden.

The typical Scandinavian snuff boxes of the first half of the nineteenth century were deep oval boxes, decorated with flat chasing or engraving, rather sketchy reminders of a long-faded Paris elegance. The central medallion has, by this time, often become no more than a formal circular motif designed to hold a set of initials, enclosed sometimes, like a Caroline coat-of-arms, with plumes of leaves or with floral sprigs. Only occasionally was the decoration varied. A full-blown, boldly drawn rose adorns a

33. Exceptionally fine engraved silver snuff box by the London makers Rawlings and Summers. Hallmarked in 1836 this box illustrates the sophistication of the best London work of the period. Sotheby's.

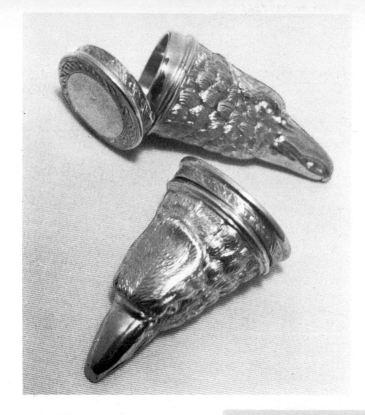

34. Tiny silver gilt form boxes in the shape of eagles' heads. Made by Nathaniel Mills. James Walker Collection.

35. Eighteenth-century cowrie shell box which has a silver lid. Also eighteenth-century silver box set with agate. James Walker collection.

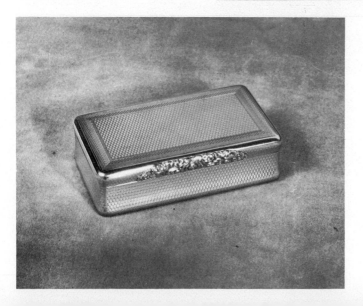

36. Fine English gold box of 1819 by London maker John Northam. Decorated with engine turning and with chased floral thumbpiece. Wartski.

37. Swiss gold box in the Louis Seize style, made about 1780 soon after the revival of enamel painting in Geneva. Christie's.

38. (top) Typical Swiss gold painted enamel box made in Geneva about 1800 with romantic scene in over-elaborate surround.

(bottom) Swiss painted enamel box of lobed oval form of 1835 with scenes by the most famous of the Geneva enamel painters Jean-Louis Richter together with Aime-Julien Troll on lid and base. This box like many of these produced at this time was made for the Turkish market. The box itself was made by A. Magnim. Christie's.

39. (a) & (b) Two pretty lobbed oval gold floral boxes decorated in painted enamels. The box on the left was produced in Geneva about 1820, the other about 1830. Christie's.

40. Plain silver canted corner box made in Finland by Johan Zettersten in 1810. National Museum, Finland.

41. One of the diplomatic snuff boxes produced in Paris for the Emperor Napoleon. This one has the unusual feature of being a musical snuff box. Christie's.

42. Glass snuff bottles decorated with painting inside. Christie's.

43. Chinese snuff bottle carved from grey agate, the dark brown inclusions carved to represent a pony tethered to a tree, with a monkey and a butterfly on the opposite side. The cover to which a spoon is attached is carved from coral. This fine bottle sold for 1,350 guineas at Christie's in 1972. Christie's.

44 & 45. (top and base of same box) (Right) Repoussé-chased silver box made in China in the nineteenth century. (Above) Detail of the repoussé chasing on the base of the box. James Walker Collection.

46. Six form boxes dating from the late eighteenth and early nineteenth century in the Pinto Collection in the Birmingham Museum.

47. Two pressed walnut boxes.
French, early nineteenth century.
The one on the left has masonic
emblems pressed into it, that on
the right depicts Henry IV of
France returning from the chase.
Many of these boxes have historical scenes. Pinto Collection, Birmingham Museum.

48. Very few gold snuff boxes are
produced nowadays. This one was
made by Stuart Devlin in 1972.
Stuart Devlin.

Swedish box of 1804, a quiver of arrows decorates another Swedish box of 1806, and another one with a heart stabbed through by two arrows is to be seen in the Göteborg Historiska Museum, but these were exceptions from the general rule.

As the century continued the oval Swedish boxes sometimes tended to become elongated, and some of them in the 1830s and 40s verged on the shuttle-shaped, like the box by Eric Söderholm in the Kunstindustrimuseet at Oslo.

Rounded oblong boxes were produced in Scandinavia in limited numbers during the second decade of the nineteenth century. Bo Bramsen illustrates a charming Swedish one, made by Isak Malmborg in 1814, with a very nice all-over chased design, and in plate 40 a perfectly plain Finnish box from National museum, Helsinki, is illustrated. A number of the Swedish gold box makers, who always seem to have been more fashion-conscious than the silver box makers, were producing gold boxes in the new style even earlier than this. There is a gold box by Edvard Nordberg made as early as 1801 in this style, decorated with alternate bands of bright- and matt-finished gold within a rope-work border. And from the second and third decades comes a series of gold boxes in this form, with an overall design in a manner which harks back to the Italian seventeenth-century boxes and the Paris boxes of the early eighteenth century. Bramsen illustrates examples of these revivalist boxes from Swedish private collections made by Olof Israel Berggren and Carl Gustaf Nyman.

The majority of surviving Scandinavian oblong boxes date, however, from the 1830s, 40s and 50s. To this period belong simple fluted boxes, rounded and oblong, indistinguishable from English boxes of the same type except for the hallmarks. The decoration on the Scandinavian chased silver boxes in this form is, however, quite different from that on the English boxes. A Norwegian box of 1845 by H. C. Lems in the Kunstindustrimuseet at Oslo well illustrates this difference. The chasing round the central oval on the lid consists of complex scroll-work again harking back to early eighteenth-century French designs. The foliate and floral motifs on the walls of the box, though they resemble those on some English boxes, are more Renaissance in character, with suggestions of the acanthus decoration intermixed with nineteenth-century rose motifs. Danish boxes from the same period are decorated with rather coarser versions of Renaissance decoration. A box by Roland Mellin of Helsinki in Finland's National Museum has rose and rose-leaf decoration against a ground chased with a matting punch, and is more typically nineteenth-century in feeling but could not have been produced in England. In a way that is difficult to describe Scandinavian roses are never quite the same as English roses.

The Scandinavian makers also produced some amusing form boxes in the middle years of the nineteenth century. Anton Michelsen of Copenhagen produced a silver box in the form of an oyster shell in 1860, Fredrik Tiander of Lovisa in Finland made one in the form of a flintlock in 1840, and like the English box makers, the Scandinavian makers continued to mount cowrie shells.

CHAPTER FOUR

NOSTALGIA AND IMPERIALISM

In France the Louis Seize style survived the revolution. Deep oval boxes continued to be made well into the nineteenth century, though riots of flowers replaced the neo-classical imagery of the originals. At the 1973 Antique Dealers Fair, Garrards showed a box made about 1820 which epitomises this none-too-happy marriage of styles. The medallion is still there in the centre of the lid, and this motif is repeated round the walls of the box as the medallion motif had often been fifty years earlier. But these nineteenth-century medallions are crammed with flowers, flowers which are too pink and too blue and too perfect, like illustrations on a seedsman's catalogue. Round the medallion on the lid is a formal floral and foliate border against a rather too pretty pink background, while the floral and foliate enamel motifs on the walls of the box are given a background part pink and part green, producing an effect as sugary as a cake. This marriage of styles can be seen again in a box in the Victoria and Albert Museum. The decoration on the lid of this box, which was probably made as late as 1840, reminds one of those beadwork wreaths so much in evidence at French funerals. The decoration is a remarkable feat of craftsmanship, however, as the central medallion, outlined by a course of rose diamonds, here again contains a riot of flowers, but three-dimensional flowers this time, the petals and leaves enamelled in soft pinks and blues and yellows and green applied to a black background and the roses given rose diamond centres. The unknown maker of this box, having imitated nature on the lid, imitated one art with another on the sides. For what appears at first sight to be niello work turns out to be a simulation of it done in enamels.

The French had swept away their traditions so violently at the end of the previous century that they now began to exhibit a nostalgia for the past. Side by side with shallow oblong engine-turned gold boxes similar to those popular across the channel in England, there were produced in Paris in the first half of the nineteenth century boxes that harked back to the middle of the eighteenth. These *en cage* boxes in the style of the Louis XV period were the work of Gabriel-Raoul Morel. Also in the middle of the century Alexandre Lefevre produced work modelled on the fashionable boxes by the great boxmakers of the 1760s. Kenneth Snowman illustrates three boxes by Morel. Morel was "a marvellous technician" and these *en cage* boxes are lavishly and beautifully made, particularly those with panels which are mosaics of richly tinted mother-of-pearl, coral and ivory, a technique known as *laque burgauté*. Yet one would detect at once that they are the work of a craftsman harking back to earlier times, even if one did not know it. What is the subtle difference between these boxes and the originals they mirror? Is it that the proportions are not quite right? Is it because the decorative details betray them? Or is it a lack of conviction that so often inhibits a man working in a manner not of his own times?

France, which had rid itself of kings and courts for a time and set its face against courtly habits, snuff-taking among them, had soon become disenchanted with revolutionary government. France had an Emperor on the throne again and in the new Imperial court circle, snuff and snuff boxes were once more very much *de rigueur*. Napoleon himself, whose Imperial pretensions led him to unsuccessfully seek to be crowned with the crown of Charlemagne, proved a great patron of the boxmakers. Like the French kings of the previous century, he showered snuff boxes on courtiers and ambassadors. Even when he was removed to Elba in 1814, he continued to play the Emperor, presenting the captain of the *Undaunted* with one of his Imperial boxes.

These Imperial boxes were usually of oblong form with rounded corners. They bore in the centre of the lid a flattering portrait of the little Corsican who had risen so high in the world (plate 41). Round this portrait were set, like a nimbus, a series of large diamonds or large pastes, depending, presumably, on the standing of the recipient for whom the box was intended or the degree of the Emperor's indebtedness. The number of these boxes which were produced is indicated by the fact that the Emperor's jeweller, Bernard-Armand Marguerit, supplied him with a hundred of them in 1806, and a further fifty in 1807, while Nitot et Fils contributed another forty-two of them.

Another type of Napoleonic Imperial box exists, one to which a scrolled initial "N" set with diamonds is applied to the lid, against either a matt background as on the box in the Victoria and Albert Museum, or against a background of deep blue enamel. It is said, incidentally, that for his own use Napoleon preferred a gold-lined tortoise-shell box with a cameo on the lid.

From nineteenth-century France have come down to us considerable numbers of tortoise-shell boxes with minimal gold mounts. A number of such boxes are to be seen in the Jewel Room at the Victoria and Albert Museum with circular mosaics mounted in the lids, one showing a view of classical Rome, another a view of Naples and a third the Forum in Rome. These mosaics are certainly Italian work imported by the Paris boxmakers, as their predecessors had once imported the work of Japanese lacquer artists. Similar mosaics were used by Italian boxmakers in the late eighteenth century and nineteenth century to decorate their lids, sometimes inlaid in the lava which is to be found in abundance on the Italian peninsula.

Other Paris-made tortoise-shell boxes from this period in the Jewel Room feature portrait miniatures, including one of the Duke of Wellington, a full length of Louis XIV and a head and shoulders of Charles I's daughter, Henrietta d'Orléans. There is also a tortoise-shell box the whole lid of which is taken up with a rather badly executed Venus with nymphs. Also among the boxes in this important collection are a number which serve to illustrate the stylistic chaos which reigned in Paris during the decades after the revolution. There is an extraordinary, but really rather effective box, made by L. A. F. Ricart about 1810, the whole lid of which is covered by a huge cabochon chalcedony, cut intaglio to depict a man driving a chariot. There is also an oblong box by the same maker, with rather lifeless foliate chasing against a matted ground on the lid and a bold relief cameo in the centre. Another maker of the period, A. A. Héguin, produced an oblong box about 1820 with a painting on mother-of-pearl on the lid. A long oblong gold box decorated with blue enamel and with a portrait of Louis XIV on the lid was made by A. J. M. Vachette in the previous decade. These boxes really seem to sum up the boxes of nineteenth-century France—the lack of unanimity on the question of style, the competent craftsmanship, but also the total lack of that inspiration which had carried the boxmaker's craft to such heights a century earlier.

CHAPTER FIVE

AUSTRIA'S LEGACY OF EXCESS

Gold snuff boxes had been produced in Vienna during the eighteenth century, though it is usually difficult to identify a box as being of Austrian origin. This is for two reasons. One is that Austrian boxes are invariably unmarked, and another is that most of the Vienna boxes were derivative in style. In Austria under Maria-Theresa all things fashionable were copied from France, while later in the century German styles were favoured; the Vienna makers copied the boxes of Neuber and these are sometimes indistinguishable from the originals.

From the Maria-Theresa period come some of the few really distinguished Vienna boxes. These were produced by an unknown goldsmith or goldsmiths, and decorated by that fine enamel painter who was at one time one of the decorators at the Meissen porcelain factory, Philipp Ernst Schindler. Schindler, like some of his contemporaries in Paris in the 1750s and 60s, was obviously impressed by the genre paintings of Teniers, and there are examples of his enamel paintings after Teniers in the Louvre collection, in the A La Vieille Russie in New York and the Victoria and Albert Museum in London. He also decorated these deep round and oval boxes in the Louis Seize form in the manner of Boucher. His draughtsmanship and the delicacy of his painting are exemplified by his decoration in a very pretty round box in the collection of the Victoria and Albert Museum. This has a circular plaque in the centre with a *grisaille* of the death of Adonis, the monochrome effect enriched by a sky rendered in a sugary pink colour. The border of the box and the walls are enriched by *basse-taille* enamelling in bright green.

Most of the other boxes in the French manner which are attributed to anonymous Viennese makers tend to be rather clumsy in conception and overloaded with ornamental detail. Those Austrian makers who produced boxes inlaid with stones in the style of Neuber often also seem to have been intent on outdoing the originals in complexity. Austrian excess is seen at its worst, however, at the end of the eighteenth century and during the nineteenth. Kenneth Snowman writes of some of these boxes,

> smothered by writhing systems of engraving or conflicting patterns of engine-turning, their clumsy lids centred by the frequently ill-painted likeness of some unattractive Hapsburg personage—these are left with us, a constant hazard to be side-stepped at public auction.[1]

Even less attractive are those boxes set with a mass of diamonds or big unconvincing pastes. There is a flat oblong box of this type, made in 1832 and now in the collection of the Metropolitan Museum in New York, with a serried row of pastes round an oval portrait, but the style at its worst was exemplified by two boxes which have appeared at Christie's salerooms in recent years. These gold boxes were very similar, both being of a clumsy bombé form, encrusted with technically accomplished but clumsy chasing, and studded with big diamonds. One has an oval portrait of a bewhiskered and bemedalled Emperor Franz Joseph on the lid encircled by two courses of diamonds. The bearded man who is the subject of the portrait on the other box is unidentified.

[1] *Ibid.*

CHAPTER SIX

RUSSIAN NINETEENTH-CENTURY BOXES

The St Petersburg court circle continued to proffer its patronage to artists and craftsmen throughout the nineteenth century, and foreign goldsmiths, most of them Germans, continued to settle in the city. Joseph Friedrich Kolb was one of these emigrant German goldsmiths who came to Russia to seek his fortune. One of his boxes is in the Walters Art Gallery in Baltimore, and it reveals him as an outstanding goldsmith. This oval box in *quatre-couleur* gold is superbly chased with military scenes within a complex border that harks back to the rococo. Another expatriate German maker was Johann Wilhelm Keibel, a lavish example of whose work is now in the Wellington Museum in London. The lid has an oval portrait of Alexander I who presented the box to the Duke of Wellington. The box is a flat oblong with cut corners, richly decorated with applied mounts set with diamonds between patterned borders of enamelwork. These flat oblong *boîtes-à-portrait* were apparently popular at this period. A rather fine example made about 1815 was sold at a Christie's sale in Geneva in 1972. This bears the portrait of an unknown general in a paste-set frame on the lid. Another common feature of these boxes is high-relief chasing against a matted ground, and on this box the chaser has depicted appropriate military trophies linked by floral and foliate motifs. Another very similar box, with a framed portrait and high-relief chasing contrasting with the matt areas, is in the Cleveland Museum of Art.

The Russian boxmakers also sometimes decorated their boxes with Swiss enamel paintings. Another appeared in the 1972 Christie's Geneva sale. One would have taken bets that this was a Swiss box. It even had a signed miniature by Richter mounted on the lid within a border of white and blue bands, dark blue circles and gilt foliage against a light blue ground. However, it bears the mark of the father of the St Petersburg maker of the Wellington box,

Otto Samuel Keibel. One can only conclude that this Russian box was in fact sent to Geneva to be decorated, for there is no record of Richter ever having gone to Russia. Another Russian box, illustrated by Clare le Corbeiller,[1] also looks as though the enamel decoration is either Swiss work or was perhaps done by a Geneva enameller who had found employment in St Petersburg. Yet another snuff box in this Swiss style was the one which Pierre Théremin produced in St Petersburg in 1800, which was included in Wartski's Thousand Years of Enamel exhibition in 1971. Another example of the Russian makers employing the work of foreign artists is the fine box in the Metropolitan Museum in New York, a round box also made by Otto Samuel Kiebel which has a Van Blarenberghe gouache mounted in the lid.

The Russian court continued to take snuff throughout the nineteenth century, but cigarette smoking gradually replaced it as a fashionable vice. The last of the great Russian court goldsmiths, Carl Fabergé, is more famous for his exquisite cigarette boxes, though he also catered for the snuff-takers of his time. It is perhaps not without significance that Fabergé, who again raised the craft of boxmaking to an art at the end of the nineteenth century in Russia, was of French origin. The Fabergés were Huguenots, and like so many of their faith they were forced to seek refuge outside their native country when Louis XIV revoked the protective Edict of Henri of Navarre. The Fabergés settled first in Germany and from there arrived eventually in St Petersburg, where Carl's father gained a considerable reputation as a court jeweller. Carl Fabergé was sent off in his teens to Germany to serve his apprenticeship, and later he travelled in France and in England. On his travels he saw some of the finest examples of the goldsmith's art, the snuff boxes of the great French makers of the eighteenth century among them.

Fabergé was obviously greatly influenced by these French boxmakers and produced a number of boxes in the French style in the years immediately after he took control of the St Petersburg business in 1870. Among these was a Louis Seize snuff box which is nothing more nor less than a pastiche of a Paris box from the middle of the eighteenth century. There is indeed a box, made by Jean François Balzae in 1754, and now in the Wartski collection,

[1] le Corbeiller, *op. cit.*

which might well have been the model for the Fabergé box. The medallion in the centre of the lid of Fabergé's box is a *grisaille* against a pink background, and there are the usual areas of enamel over engine-turning. Foliate enamel motifs and translucent beads decorate the borders, and architectural motifs divide the enamel panels on the walls of the box.

A box which Fabergé created for the Duke of Devonshire also harks back to French originals, for this tall oblong box with cut corners has an enamelled view of Chatsworth on lid and base, reminding one irresistibly of the Choiseul boxes for which Van Blarenberghe painted the gouaches. The box itself is very similar to a box, also decorated with "views", made by Jean-Joseph Barrière late in the 1770s.

Fabergé also harked back to the Imperial German style in his early period as, for example, when he produced an Imperial presentation box, which is now in the possession of the Queen Mother. This has an oval portrait of Nicholas II in a diamond-set frame with the Tsar's crowned cypher above. To this pastiche, which may or may not have been designed as a snuff box, Fabergé added his own personal contribution by laying pale mauve translucent enamel over moiré engine-turning. Such exquisite enamelling over engine-turning was one of the hallmarks of the work that emanated from Fabergé's workshops.

Fabergé gradually developed his own style, however, and began producing work in which French influence lingers only as a faint echo of the past. We see the essential Fabergé in an oval snuff box, produced presumably for the Tsar, for it has a green gold Imperial eagle in the centre of the lid. This box is an example of Fabergé's love affair with decorative minerals and of his ability to use them with unrivalled felicity. The lid and body of this box were carved from a dappled grey agate that has an effect that looks like the first raindrops on a pavement. Dividing lid and body are narrow and unobtrusive green gold mounts chased with a delicate leaf pattern, and a thumbpiece set with a single diamond is a final touch of opulence to what must be the most exquisite snuff box made in the late nineteenth century.

PART FOUR

CHAPTER ONE

CHINESE SNUFF BOTTLES

The Chinese snuff bottles are as beautiful, in their own way, as the eighteenth-century French gold boxes. The classic snuff bottle is a tiny flat-sided jar about 5 cm. high. The mouth of this short-necked jar is stopped with a cork attached to a domed lid. From this cork depends a miniature scoop, similar in form to a marrow scoop, with which the snuff was removed. These bottles were made in an incredible variety of materials and decorated in a bewilderment of styles, over a period of some two centuries.

All who are interested in these charming little vessels owe an enormous debt to Hugh H. Moss, whose years of research have recently culminated in two authoritative and superbly illustrated books—*Snuff Bottles of China*[1] and *Chinese Snuff Bottles of the Silica or Quartz Group*.[2] Hugh Moss has answered many of the questions which these intriguing bottles prompted, and I am personally indebted to him for some of the information included in this chapter.

When snuff-taking was introduced into China is not known, but Wang Shih-chên in 1705 wrote of tobacco arriving in Peking, where "it is made into snuff, which is said can clear the eyes; even more, it has the property of banishing infection". He goes on also to inform us that: "glass bottles of all and every shape and colour are made to contain it . . . They are things of great delight. There is an ivory spoon which is returned to the flask after sniffing. . . ." The existence of these containers suggests that the habit of snuffing was already well established by this time, at least in the area of Peking.

Hugh Moss believes that even at the beginning of the eighteenth century the habit was, however, still very much of a courtly one

[1] Moss, Hugh H., *Snuff Bottles of China*, London, 1971.
[2] Moss, Hugh H., *Chinese Snuff Bottles of the Silica or Quartz Group*, London, 1971.

and was restricted to Northern China. It was only towards the end of the century that snuffing spread throughout that vast country and became a general addiction.

By the end of the eighteenth century snuff-bottle collecting, as well as snuffing, was becoming a national pastime in China, and snuff bottles were regarded as the perfect gift for all occasions in the same way that boxes were in eighteenth-century Europe. A certain corrupt minister of the Ch'ien-lung dynasty had acquired by the time he died a collection of no fewer than 2,390 snuff bottles, many of which were probably gifts designed to elicit his support.

The Chinese continued to make snuff bottles up to 1912 when the Ch'ing dynasty fell and a period of chaos followed. In the 1950s, however, the Communists revived the craft and these bottles are again being made in China today, with workshops set up in Hong Kong to cater to the demand resulting from a steadily growing interest in this curious art form. It must be said that one of the problems in writing about Chinese snuff bottles is that they are extremely difficult to date. Only the "painted inside" bottles are signed and dated. The others can only be allocated to a period on the evidence of style, material and technique, and often a particular bottle could have been produced at any time during a century or more.

The earliest bottles were, as the quotation from Wang Shih-chên suggests, almost certainly glass ones, probably plain or surface-decorated with simple patterns. Then some time about the end of the third decade of the eighteenth century the Chinese glass workers developed the fascinating technique of fusing coloured glass onto the body of the bottles and carving this overlay. They depicted in this way those lively animals, those delicate leaf sprays, those flower groups, and those flittering fish which the Chinese artists handle with such mastery and subtlety in all mediums. The bottles which were decorated in this way were usually blown from milky white glass, though coloured bottles were also used. The most popular overlays were of red or green glass. Sometimes, however, multi-colour overlays were fused on to the body, either as separate blobs of glass or laid one on top of another. As many as eight colours of glass might be applied to a bottle, as is illustrated by the white bottle decorated with flowers and birds which was sold at a famous sale at Christie's in 1972, when an entire collection, and a very representative one, came up for auction. Another bottle in this sale, a blue one, was first carved and then red and black glass was fused on and carved in turn to depict on one side a man crossing a bridge and on the other, a fisherman in a boat.

A similar effect to that achieved by the glass workers was obtained by carving multi-coloured tourmaline crystals, polychromatic crystals being a common phenomenon of this material. This use of tourmaline was illustrated by a bottle in that same Christie's sale. It showed a seated figure carved on the front and dragons on the shoulders, one of them carved out of the pink area of the crystal.

Overlays were not by any means the only way in which glass bottles were decorated. Glass was enamelled with delicate flower and leaf designs, or with those still and silent landscapes which the Chinese water colour painters produced with a few deftly applied washes. Plate 42 shows examples of the "painting inside" technique, which dates from the early nineteenth century. Bottles were painted on the interior surfaces, the artist inserting his brushes through the mouth of the vessel and drawing the designs in reverse, which is something obviously easier said than done. As technical *tours de force* these bottles are very impressive, but as art they are somewhat decadent. The subjects chosen and the style of representation are what might be called Chinese neo-classical. Some are charming, but many of them are rather hackneyed.

The Chinese carved snuff bottles out of many different minerals and organic materials from the middle of the eighteenth century onwards. The stone-carvers sometimes departed from the classic form of the snuff bottle to produce fancy shapes, bottles in the shape of gourds, of fruit or vegetables, and of animals or fish. In that memorable Christie's sale there was a quartz crystal bottle in the form of a bat, an agate bottle in the form of a corn cob and a bloodstone bottle in the shape of a pomegranate, the stem composed of crystal. In the Hugh Moss collection there is a cornelian bottle carved to represent three butterflies, a jade bottle representing a dragon-carp, and another jade bottle shaped like a pig.

Jade, hardly surprisingly, was one of the favoured materials of those who carved snuff bottles from minerals. The Chinese have been carving jade since neolithic times. In the early days they used nephrite, a strong fibrous material that was also used for tools and weapons. Later the more colourful jadeite, found in Burma, was imported and both types have been carved over many centuries. Jadeite bottles are often completely plain depending on their colour and their perfect proportions for their appeal. Nephrite bottles, on the other hand, are usually decorated with incised carving or carving in relief. It is not uncommon for nephrite to have areas of alien colour in it, the mutton fat white material often exhibiting a rusty red stain, for instance. The Chinese glyptic artists have always been masters at exploiting such accidents of nature. They cut away the stone to leave the red areas standing proud, and then with drills transformed these relief areas into fruit and flowers and animals, the effect being similar to that achieved by the glass overlay technique. A very lively nephrite bottle in the Hugh Moss collection has a white body, and the intrusive grey areas have been carved with the figures of two men, one of whom is fighting with a tiger.

This same technique of using multi-coloured material to produce cameo effects is also a feature of many of the bottles carved from agates and the other chalcedonies. Agate with its banding of various colours is particularly well suited to producing this kind of decoration. A charming bottle of this type is illustrated in plate 43. It shows a monkey tethering a horse to a pine tree carved from the deep brown areas contrasting with the pale grey background. The lid is of coral carved with a Kuei dragon.

One does wonder, incidentally, about some of the lids on these bottles which look as though they really were not designed for them. Even the impeccable Chinese were presumably not invariably infallible in the matter of colour blending, but these little lids were probably often lost and could easily have been broken, and some of those which look out of character with the bottle could presumably be replacements.

Besides using the massive, or microcrystalline, quartzes the Chinese made very effective use of various coloured crystalline quartzes, and colourless transparent quartz crystal. Some of the colourless quartz crystal bottles are absolutely plain, others are carved in low relief with repeat patterns and sprigs of foliage or occasionally with representations of figures, birds and animals.

Quartz crystal bottles were sometimes also painted inside. Among the most effective of all snuff bottles were those carved from the rutilated quartzes, quartz crystal with sheaves of black hair-like tourmaline inclusions or the red, gold or silver needles of rutile. Brown crystalline quartzes were used too, including the almost black morion and the yellow citrine. The Chinese carved the rich purple amethyst as well, and the massive translucent rose quartz, and apple-green chrysoprase.

The Chinese carvers' sensitivity to the material in which they were working is revealed by the way they used these different quartzes. They tended to carve the paler materials delicately, and they increased the dramatic quality of the darker coloured crystals by heavier carving and stronger motifs. A feature of a number of the quartz bottles, incidentally, are carved false ring handles on the shoulders, simulating the handles commonly found on larger Chinese vessels.

Other hard stones used for snuff bottles include turquoise matrix, malachite, lapis lazuli and ruby matrix, all of which would have had to be imported into China from neighbouring countries. The Chinese carved the less durable stones into bottles too. They used calcite, limestone, puddingstone and bowenite serpentine. This last has been much used in recent years as a jade simulant, and "jade" snuff bottles have been carved from it.

Some of the most beautiful bottles were carved from pink coral. Hugh Moss's collection includes, for instance, a superb little coral bottle dating from 1761. Carved on the front is a phoenix in a landscape with peonies. On the reverse are the decorative characters of a little poem which tells of a bird of good omen basking amidst the peonies of a heavenly garden. Another coral bottle, a little round one made some time between 1850 and 1949, has a plump-faced man in high relief perched on the side, fishing for a toad with a coin on a piece of string. A similar bottle in the Christie's sale has a boy on the side playing with two cats.

Equally attractive are the ivory bottles, some quite plain, some intricately incised, some with areas stained with black lacquer and with the design delineated in fine lacquered lines. Then there are those bottles carved from the most unlikely organic materials. One recalls a peach carved from bamboo, a flat flask of coconut shell, a peachstone carved with figures in a landscape with buildings and trees in quite incredible detail. Small gourds were dried and used for snuff in their natural form. Gourds were also carved and sometimes had decoration pressed into the sides of them, in the same way that European wooden and horn snuff boxes had decoration pressed into their lids.

As might be expected, a nation with a centuries old ceramic tradition inevitably produced many porcelain snuff bottles. The only surprising thing is that these do not seem to have appeared before the later years of the eighteenth century. Most of the porcelain bottles are believed to have come from Imperial kilns at Ching-tê-chên which supplied the court with hordes of plates, dishes, bowls and vases. Some of these bottles had the decoration applied to them in the moulds in which they were made. Others had the relief decoration carved into the body of the bottle after it was made. The painting on the bottles was either achieved by enamelling over the glaze, or by underglaze painting, which is the technique used for most European painted ceramics. Some of the moulded bottles were obviously intended to imitate those made in natural materials such as ivory, lapis lazuli, jade and coral. Moulded bottles also simulated plants and other natural objects. In the Christie's sale there was a moulded bottle in the form of the curious finger citrus, while another was in the likeness of a golden corn cob. In the Hugh Moss collection there are white porcelain bottles moulded to represent a squirrel and a cheerful little Buddhist lion. On others dragons writhe down the length of the bottle. The subjects of the overglaze enamels and underglaze paintings will be familiar to anyone who has studied Chinese ceramics. Birds and animals in idealised landscapes, men going about their daily tasks, sprays of blossom, dragons and formalised floral motifs are delineated in those delicate tones, and with that economy of line to which only a Chinese artist could attain.

The Chinese lacquer artists also decorated snuff bottles, using the characteristic cinebar red lacquer to produce reliefs of figure groups. Delightful as these are they are far inferior to the best Japanese lacquers of the eighteenth century.

A few gold snuff bottles have been produced in China, and one of fairly recent date, one suspects, was in that Christie's sale in 1972. Bottles also were cast in copper and painted in enamels, the Asiatic equivalents of the Staffordshire painted enamel snuff boxes, though the Chinese enamelling is of incomparably higher quality.

It can be appreciated from this necessarily brief survey of a diverse and complicated art that Chinese snuff bottles are a collector's paradise. It is only fairly recently that these little bottles have been widely appreciated, and the recent growth of interest in them has inevitably had a dramatic effect on prices. The collection of 194 bottles, the sale of which at Christie's has been referred to, fetched £26,619, with individual bottles selling for as much as 500 guineas for a glass overlay bottle and 340 guineas for a carved coral one. But these prices do not seem excessive when one considers how beautiful these bottles are.

A CHINESE SILVER SNUFF BOX

There is a very curious snuff box in the James Walker collection which is illustrated in plate 44. This silver box is believed to have been made in China for export to Europe possibly in the eighteenth century but probably considerably later. It is a very accomplished piece of silversmithing; the Chinese scenes, so very different in feeling from European chinoiseries, are skilfully chased as are the decorative borders, and the box is well constructed. So far as I can discover nothing is known about any Chinese workshops producing boxes of this kind, yet it seems inconceivable that such practised craftsmanship would have produced only this one example. Such enigmas are not uncommon in the history of the crafts; craftsmanship is so taken for granted in its own time that seldom does anyone feel that the craftsman and his skills are worth mentioning.

CHAPTER TWO

WOODEN SNUFF BOXES

The inherent problem of assigning a wooden box to a particular date or a country of origin is made the more difficult by the fact that most of these boxes were produced by country craftsmen for country people. Not having to cater to fashionable customers, the men who made them paid little regard to what shapes were currently in vogue or what the latest fads of decoration were in London and Paris. Most wooden snuff boxes are pretty basic containers, and their decoration, when it exists, displays a coarse country humour or a rather naïve ingenuity. Some masquerade as pigs, or shoes or as a pair of bellows; others were made in the shape of a coffin. Some of these little coffins even contained a skeleton carved from bone, and the snuff the owner placed around this was a macabre reminder of the dust to which we all return.

Wooden snuff boxes which can with certainty be said to date from the seventeenth century or the early eighteenth are few and far between. There are, however, a few boxes in the Edward Pinto collection in the Birmingham Museum which were probably made before, or soon after, 1700. There is, for instance, an oval box with a carved device of a greyhound and three birds in the centre, which actually has "Fecit 1664" boldly carved on the lid. One is always a little suspicious of antiques that state their age, but this box appears in fact as old as it declares itself to be. In this collection there are also three very similar boxes with engine-turned abstract decoration on the lids. One of them has a silver rim and is said to be English. It is given a tentative, and one would think too early date of 1625. The gallery indeed concede in their description that engine-turning was not introduced into England from France until thirty years later than this.

Also in this very comprehensive collection is a shallow oval box ascribed to 1706. This looks absolutely in period, with its formal bone inlays. Four of these, in the form of shells, quarter the box and have inscribed in them the motto "for you the best is not too good", which is probably not contemporary. Aside from these boxes and a few in other collections, existing wooden snuff boxes all date from the middle of the eighteenth century and later.

Only a few of these later wooden boxes aspire to elegance. An oblong one with incurved sides made in burr-walnut, which Edward Pinto found during his lifetime quest for interesting and unusual woodwares, is exceptional in being as beautifully made as it was fashionable of form. It was produced, possibly in France, in the middle of the eighteenth century. Fashionable too in its day was an oval box with an inlay of boxwood and mother-of-pearl in the fan form which is one of the hallmarks of Sheraton furniture. One thinks further in this context of a little oblong birch box, hinged on the lid and possibly Scandinavian. This is decorated in neo-classical style though the medallion in the centre is no neo-Roman relief, but shows a dog receiving a bone from his mistress.

Apart from a few polished examples of the woodworker's art such as these, the best that can be said about most wooden snuff boxes is that they are interesting or perhaps "quaint". Amongst the quaint one would definitely include the form boxes in the Pinto collection. Aside from those macabre coffin boxes, there were other salutary reminders of the inevitable approaching end of life, in the form of skulls with hinged crowns. Other form boxes include one in the shape of a carpenter's plane made in beech and there is a German nineteenth-century box beautifully carved in the form of the hull of a ship. There are a number of boxes of book form, including one little one with silver inlays which could have been made in the early eighteenth or even the late seventeenth century. There are two boxes in the form of hands, one from the eighteenth and one from the nineteenth centuries—the owners of which lifted the thumb by the nail to get at his snuff. There are, too, a number of examples of animal boxes. Apart from a poor pig, and a hardly less poor bull-dog, there is a rather fine fish box and an amusing frog carved from burr-maple (see plate 46).

Occasionally wooden boxes had lids carved with contemporary scenes, like one which shows a customer being served in a haberdasher's shop. Another form of lid decoration was a mosaic, and these intricate compositions in tessellae were probably of Italian origin. Karel Citroen has a tortoise-shell box in his collection with a hard stone mosaic depicting a black and white rabbit munching herbage, very similar in style and technique to those occasionally found on wooden boxes. The Citroen box is signed "Giacomo Raffaelli" and dated 1791. Stickwork boxes, produced by gluing together rods of different coloured woods and slicing the resulting block to produce mock mosaics, were made in Tunbridge Wells in the nineteenth century.

Among the most interesting and the most sophisticated of wooden snuff boxes were those French ones with pressed decoration on their lids. An early example is in the British Museum and depicts the two great French philosophers, Voltaire and Rousseau, in profile facing each other. The two men died in the same year, 1778, and the box was believed to have been sold as a *momento mori*. One does not have to go further than the Birmingham Museum to see a really representative collection of these fine round maple boxes with pressed inserts in the lids, made in France between 1800 and about 1820 (see plate 47). The medallions which decorate these boxes were made by pressing thin sections of burr-maple between steel dies to produce a high-relief design. The detail was sometimes sharpened by subsequent carving, as repoussé decoration on metal is improved by chasing. A medallion when complete was set into a turned maple lid, which fitted a similarly turned body that was usually lined with tortoise-shell. The subjects depicted on these lids include historical characters like Henry IV and Cardinal Mazarin, and it is interesting to recall that Obrisset, who had pressed horn in a similar way a century earlier, had also illustrated historical subjects. Some French boxes bear contemporary portraits, Napoleon's inevitably, but also the English Prince Regent. One medallion in the Birmingham collection depicts a romantic Swiss landscape—Lac Léman with its mountainous backdrop. There are, too, those heads which look sad if turned one way and happy when turned the other. There is a box with three views of a skull on it divided into numbered segments, produced in honour of the noted phrenologist, Dr Franz Gall. There are scenes of village merrymaking, a Susannah and the Elders, Joan of Arc tied to the stake on top of bundles of faggots, along with some mildly erotic boxes. One shows a girl losing her balance on a see-saw and displaying comely thighs, and another depicts a young man clambering through his mistress's window, in search of pleasure. These "licentious" scenes are, however, a far cry from those "lustful postures" which adorned the inner lids of English, German and Swiss boxes carried by the rakes and fops of the eighteenth century.

Scotland produced a great many wooden boxes in the nineteenth century decorated with tartans. The wearing of the plaid had been prohibited in Scotland after the 1745 rising, but this prohibition had been relaxed towards the end of the eighteenth century. By the beginning of the nineteenth century the tartan had become fashionable, a reassertion of Scottish nationalism. In the 1820s a legless man in Perthshire began to produce rather crude whitewood snuff boxes, the lids decorated with tartan patterns drawn in Indian inks and protected with varnish. From such inauspicious beginnings a thriving industry developed. The idea was taken up by the brothers William and Andrew Smith of Mauchline in Ayrshire, which is Burns country, and they were known for their Burns boxes as well as the tartan boxes. The Smiths had competitors, including Clark and Davidson who made neo-Jacobite boxes with portraits of Bonny Prince Charlie inside the lids, and Davidson, Wilson and Amphlet who boasted of the patronage they received from William IV and Queen Victoria.

By 1832 the Smiths were employing a hundred men making tartan souvenirs, including snuff boxes, made from the light and smooth wood of the sycamore and lined with tin. These so-called Laurencekirk boxes were very well constructed. They were put together from as many as twenty-six components and their hinges were hand carved with surprising precision. A system of mechanical pens were used to delineate the colourful tartans on the lids of the Laurencekirk boxes at first, but later the patterns were rolled on or applied by a lithographic process. As well as being decorated with tartans, some of these boxes were also decorated with Highland scenes, romantic Scottish castles or copies of Landseer's paintings, done in oils by artists who received perhaps thirty shillings a week for their work.

Clare le Corbeiller illustrates a fine example from an American private collection with a painting of the "Cotter's Saturday night" on the lid, within a surround of incised oak leaves. Another of the firm's specialities were the so-called Scoto-Russian boxes, made to imitate the niello-decorated silver boxes of Russian origin. These wooden boxes made at Mauchline by William and Andrew Smith, were covered with tin foil which was painted and then the metal was scribed to produce bright areas to simulate silver.

Russia, incidentally, is one of the main sources of the inexpensive wooden boxes that many of today's snuffers use. They export, among others, little rounded oblong boxes, hinged on the top and carved from birch and varnished—hardly works of art, but workmanlike and inexpensive containers.

SELECT BIBLIOGRAPHY

Batsford, B. J. and Jackson, *An Illustrated History of English Plate*, Country Life, 1911.

Berry-Hill, Henry and Sidney, *Antique Gold Boxes*, New York, 1960.

Bramsen, Bo, *Nordiske Snusdasen*, Politikensforlag, 1965.

le Corbeiller, Clare, *European and American Snuff Boxes*, London, 1966.

Delieb, Eric, *Investing in Silver*, Barrie and Rockcliff, 1967.

Delieb, Eric, *Silver Boxes*, Herbert Jenkins, 1968.

Dent, Herbert C., *Piqué, A Beautiful Minor Art*, London, 1923.

Evans, George, *The Old Snuff House of Fribourg and Treyer*. Privately printed in London, 1961.

Evans, Joan, *A History of Jewellery*, London, 1953.

Honey, W. B., *German Porcelain*, London, 1947.

Honey, W. B., *European Ceramic Art*, London, 1949.

Hughes, G. Bernard, *English Snuff Boxes*, London 1971.

Hughes, G. Bernard and Therle, *English Painted Enamels*, London, 1951.

Jackson, Sir Charles, *English Goldsmiths and Their Marks*, London, 1921.

McCausland, Hugh, *Snuff and Snuff Boxes*, London, 1951.

Mitford, Nancy, *The Sun King*, Hamish Hamilton, 1966.

Moss, Hugh H., *Chinese Snuff Bottles of the Silica and Quartz Group*, London, 1971.

Moss, Hugh H., *Snuff Bottles of China*, London, 1971.

Nocq and Dreyfus, *Tabatières, Boîtes et Etuis*, Paris, 1930.

Nocq, Henry, *Le Poinçon de Paris*, Paris, 1926.

Norton, Richard and Martin, *A History of Gold Snuff Boxes*, London, 1938.

Phillips, Philip A. S., *John Obrisset: His Work in Horn and Tortoiseshell*, London, 1931.

Pinto, Edward H., *Wooden Bygones of Smoking and Snuff-Taking*, London, 1961.

Snowman, Kenneth, *Eighteenth-Century Gold Boxes of Europe*, London, 1966.

INDEX

Unless otherwise stated, plate numbers refer to black and white plates